Knowledge Management for Services, Operations and Manufacturing

CHANDOS
KNOWLEDGE MANAGEMENT SERIES

Series Editor: Melinda Taylor
(email: melindataylor@chandospublishing.com)

Chandos' new series of books are aimed at all those individuals interested in knowledge management. They have been specially commissioned to provide the reader with an authoritative view of current thinking. If you would like a full listing of current and forthcoming titles, please visit our web site www.chandospublishing. com or contact Hannah Grace-Williams on email info@chandospublishing.com or telephone number +44 (0) 1993 848726.

New authors: we are always pleased to receive ideas for new titles; if you would like to write a book for Chandos, please contact Dr Glyn Jones on email gjones@ chandospublishing.com or telephone number +44 (0) 1993 848726.

Bulk orders: some organisations buy a number of copies of our books. If you are interested in doing this, we would be pleased to discuss a discount. Please contact Hannah Grace-Williams on email info@chandospublishing.com or telephone number +44 (0) 1993 848726.

Knowledge Management for Services, Operations and Manufacturing

Tom Young

Chandos Publishing

Oxford · England

Chandos Publishing (Oxford) Limited
TBAC Business Centre
Avenue 4
Station Lane
Witney
Oxford OX28 4BN
UK
Tel: +44 (0) 1993 848726 Fax: +44 (0)1865 884448
Email: info@chandospublishing.com
www.chandospublishing.com

First published in Great Britain in 2008

ISBN:
978 1 84334 324 0 (paperback)
978 1 84334 325 7 (hardback)
1 84334 324 X (paperback)
1 84334 325 8 (hardback)

British Library Cataloguing-in-Publication Data.
A catalogue record for this book is available from the British Library.

Typeset by Avocet Typeset, Chilton, Aylesbury, Bucks.
Printed in the UK and USA.

Contents

Acknowledgements   *ix*

List of figures and tables   *xi*

About the author   *xiii*

Introduction   *xv*

1 Principles   1

   Introduction   1

   What is knowledge?   2

   Tacit and explicit knowledge   4

   What is knowledge management?   5

2 Knowledge management models for services, operations and manufacturing   9

3 Performance benchmarking and knowledge management   13

   Target setting   16

   What knowledge   17

4 Processes for learning from performance   21

   After action review   21

   Performance learning review   25

5 Processes for learning from others   31

   Peer assist   31

   Site knowledge visit   34

   Knowledge exchange   45

   Business driven action learning   60

6	**Communities of practice**	**65**
	Communities of purpose	68
	Communities of practice	68
	Community of interest	71
	Community tools and processes	71
7	**The corporate knowledge base**	**73**
8	**Technology**	**79**
	Portals, or knowledge libraries	79
	Lessons learned databases	81
	Yellow pages/people finders	84
	eLearning	86
	Community question and answer forums	87
	Blogs	90
	Wikis	91
9	**Roles**	**93**
	Corporate knowledge manager	94
	Business knowledge manager	95
	knowledge management sponsor	95
	knowledge management coach	96
	Community facilitator	96
	Subject matter experts	97
	Librarians and cybrarians	98
	Roles in a legal services context	98
	The roles of operations technicians in knowledge management	100
10	**Assurance and monitoring**	**103**
	Knowledge management standards	103
	Knowledge management plans	104
	Knowledge management monitoring	105
	Knowledge management metrics	106

11 The linkage with other management disciplines   107

Six sigma   107

Lean operations   109

Quality management, total quality management
and quality circles   111

Risk management   113

Health, safety and environmental management   115

Performance management   116

12 Case histories   119

BBC Production and Services   119

BP's Operations Value Process (OVP)   130

Knowledge Management at CfBT Education Trust   133

General Motors   142

Orange   165

13 Summary and conclusions   181

Strategy   181

Communities of practice   181

Review   182

Benchmark   182

Learn   182

Do   183

Roles   183

Assurance and monitoring   183

References   185

Appendix 1

Forthcoming publications   187

Index   *189*

Acknowledgments

I would like to thank my business partner, Nick Milton, for all his support. I would also like to thank those people who contributed the case studies, and also those who spent time talking and sharing their experiences with me. Finally, I want to say thanks to my Mum and Dad, Helen, my wife, and Thomas our son.

List of figures and tables

Figures

1.1	The data – information – knowledge – action link	3
1.2	The varying codifiability of knowledge	6
2.1	Knowledgement model for services, operations and manufacturing	10
2.2	Knowledge management activities	11
3.1	Four linked performance management activities	14
3.2	Cost performance example	14
3.3	Categorisation of types of knowledge at company level	18
3.4	Categorisation of types of knowledge at unit level	20
4.1	Flipchart marked up for an after action review	23
12.1	The BBC 'windmill' diagram	121
12.2	Staircase diagram	132
12.3	Balanced scorecard	137
12.4	CfBT Education Trust Corporate Learning intranet	140
12.5	GM Product Best Practice Structure	148

12.6   Graphical Domain View example   150
12.7   GM Product Best Practice Meter Stack   153
12.8   Facilitated best practice collaboration process   154
12.9   Knowledge set   155
12.10   Best practice and knowledge set annual
         overall metrics   160
12.11   Annual number of best practices viewed by
         global region   161
12.12   Number of best practices viewed by authors
         and users in 2006   161
12.13   Normalized 36MIS Actual Warranty and
         Warranty Forecast   163
12.14   The knowledge benefits tree   172
12.15   Customer satisfaction metrics   178

Tables

5.1   Knowledge needs and knowledge offers   51
6.1   Comparison of communities   67
12.1   Six elements and 26 key practices   131
12.2   Technical memory – best practice annual
         metrics   160

About the author

Tom specialises in assisting senior management to articulate the benefits of systematically managing the knowledge of their organisation. His value-adding approach not only stimulates thought but challenges 'the way we do business around here'. He is a highly respected facilitator and coach. Tom is one of a very small group of individuals who have the proven capability to take a knowledge management programme from strategy development in the boardroom all the way to frontline implementation. Tom is a Chartered Engineer and had an early career in manufacturing and new product development. He then made the transition back into the oil industry and moved towards the business side of the industry, formalised this with an MBA and becoming a business manager with BP. Business re-engineering roles in internal audit prepared him for the award winning Virtual Teamworking Project and eventually to become a founding member of the BP Knowledge Management Team.

Tom now chairs Knoco Ltd. He has a global perspective and extensive experience of assisting companies to prepare business cases to support the introduction of their knowledge management programme. He is a Chamber of Commerce Past President.

Tom is married to Helen and they have a son Thomas. Tom is based in Scotland and is frequently to be found fly fishing on one of the local lochs.

Introduction

The purpose of this book is to share some of our learning on how knowledge management can be and is applied in service industries, in manufacturing, and in continuous operations and production. The book describes theory and models for knowledge management in an operational setting, and contains case studies from a number of service, operational and manufacturing industries.

This book is intended to complement the book *Knowledge Management for Teams and Projects* by Nick Milton, which addressed the application of knowledge management to discrete project-based activity.

Principles

This introductory chapter is also included in the sister volume *Knowledge Management for Teams and Projects* by Nick Milton.

Introduction

It is traditional to start a book of this type with the discussion of 'What is knowledge?', and 'What is knowledge management?'. If you are already quite clear about the distinction, then this section is not for you. However, there is often still some confusion over the definitions of, and fuzzy boundaries between, knowledge management, information management and data management. The latter two disciplines are well established; people know what they mean, people are trained in them, and there are plenty of reference books to explain what they are and how they work. Knowledge management, on the other hand, is a relatively new term, and one that requires a little bit of explanation.

I will start by looking at 'What Is knowledge?'.

What is knowledge?

Knowledge is something that only humans can possess. People know things; computers can't know things. Traditionally, in our schooling system and in many organisations, knowledge is seen as a personal possession. If you are a knowledgeable person, you have status and you are in demand. Knowledge gives you the ability to take action. Knowledge is based on experience, it requires information, and it involves the application of theory or heuristic (either consciously or unconsciously), and it allows you to make knowledgeable decisions. Knowledge has something that data and information lack, and those extra ingredients are the experience and the heuristics.

As an illustration, consider the link between data, information and knowledge as they are involved in decision-making in a mining exploration company.

The company pays for a mineralogy survey, taking samples across an area of mountainous country. Each sample is analysed, and each is a data point. These data are held in a database.

In order for these data to be interpreted, they need to be presented in a meaningful way. The company uses a Geographical Information System to present the data in map form. A contour map of the mineralogical data represents information, showing the pattern of changes in the mineralogy across the mountain belt.

However, this map needs to be interpreted. Such information, even presented in map form, is meaningless to the layman, but an experienced mining geologist can look at it, apply his or her experience, use some theory, heuristics or rules of thumb, and can make a decision. That decision may be to conduct some further sampling, to open a mine, or to dismiss the area as unprospective.

The mining geologist has 'know-how' – he or she knows how to interpret contour maps of mineralogical data. It can use that knowledge to take information (presented in the map), and decide which action to take. That know-how is developed from training, from years of experience, through the acquisition of a set of heuristics and working models, and through many conference and bar-room conversations with the wider community of mining geologists.

Figure 1.1 The data – information – knowledge – action link

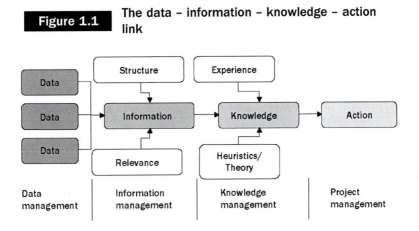

Knowledge that leads to action is 'know-how'. Your experience, and the theories and heuristics to which you have access, allows you to know what to do, and to know how to do it. In this book, you can use the terms 'knowledge' and 'know-how' interchangeably.

In large organisations, irrespective of whether it's an operational, production or service environment, knowledge and know-how are increasingly being seen as a communal possession, rather than an individual possession. Communities of practice (see Chapter 6) are networks of people who have collective ownership of knowledge. Such knowledge is 'common knowledge' – the things that 'everybody knows'. This common knowledge is based on shared experiences, and on collective theory and heuristics that are defined, agreed and validated by the community.

Shared experience is often hard to codify, and is transferred within an operational, production or service environment by communication and learning meetings, and between locations by processes such as peer assist, technical limit, optioneering and action learning (all of which are described in this book). The theories and heuristics can be written down and codified into case histories, lessons learned, project best practices, and (ultimately) company policies and standards. This codification process will be described later.

Tacit and explicit knowledge

The terms tacit and explicit are often used when talking about knowledge. The original authors, Nonaka and Takeuchi (1995) use these terms to define 'unable to be expressed' and 'able to be expressed' respectively. Thus tacit knowledge, in the original usage, means knowledge held instinctively, in the unconscious mind and in the muscle memory, which cannot be transferred in words alone. Knowledge of how to ride a bicycle, for example, is tacit knowledge, as it is almost impossible to explain verbally.

Nowadays these original definitions have become blurred, and tacit and explicit are often used to describe 'knowledge that has not been codified' and 'knowledge that has been codified' (or 'head knowledge' and 'recorded knowledge' respectively). This latter definition is a more useful one in the context of knowledge management within operational, service or production environments, as it defines knowledge based on where it exists, rather than on its intrinsic codifiability. So knowledge that exists only in people's heads is termed tacit knowledge, and knowledge that has been recorded somewhere is termed explicit knowledge.

The importance to an organisation of addressing both tacit and explicit knowledge is emphasised in the General Motors case history in Chapter 12.

There is a wide range of types of knowledge, from easily codifiable to completely uncodifiable. Some know-how, such as 'how to cook a pizza', can be codified and written down, and most households contain codified cooking knowledge (cookery books). Other know-how, such as how to ride a bicycle, cannot be codified, and there would be no point in trying to teach someone to ride a bike by giving them a book on the subject. Operational, production and service knowledge sits in the middle of Figure 1.2. Some of it can be codified, some can't. Some can be captured and made explicit, some can't. This assertion has implications for how operational knowledge will be managed, because it means we need to address both the tacit and explicit dimensions.

What is knowledge management?

If knowledge is a combination of experience, theory and heuristics, developed by an individual or a community of practice, which allows decisions to be made and correct actions to be taken, then what is knowledge management? Larry Prusak, of McKinsey Consulting, says 'It is the attempt to recognise what is essentially a human asset buried in the minds of individuals, and leverage it into a corporate asset that can be used by a broader set of individuals, on whose decisions the firm depends'. Larry is here suggesting that the shift from seeing knowledge as

Figure 1.2	The varying codifiability of knowledge. Some tasks (such as cooking, or constructing a garden shed) are relatively simple and easily codifiable. Others may be quite simple (riding a bike), but very hard to codify

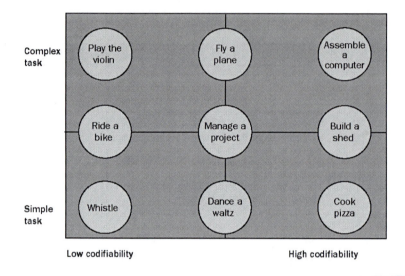

personal property, to seeing knowledge as communal property, is at the heart of knowledge management. To ensure management discipline, we need to make sure that this is done systematically, routinely and in the service of business strategy.

Gorelick *et al.* (2004) suggest that 'Knowledge Management is fundamentally a systematic approach for optimising the access, for individuals and teams within an organisation, to relevant actionable advice, knowledge and experience from elsewhere'. This definition is similar to that of Prusak, although it looks at knowledge from the point of view of the knowledge user rather than the knowledge supplier. It also emphasises the need for the knowledge to be relevant and actionable, and therefore valuable to the knowledge user.

If you read widely about knowledge management, or attend many of the conferences, you will discover that for many people, 'knowledge management' is currently not a popular term. Some people challenge whether knowledge could ever be managed. They point to the intangible tacit nature of knowledge, the difficulty of separating knowledge from people, the difficulty of measuring the flow of knowledge, and suggest that this makes knowledge effectively unmanageable. Terms such as 'knowledge sharing', 'systematic learning' and 'shared learning' are often proposed instead.

However, modern businesses are becoming increasingly familiar with the practice of managing intangibles. Risk management, customer relations management, safety management and brand management are all recognised management approaches. Knowledge is not significantly less tangible or measurable than risk, brand, or safety, and the term 'management' suggests a healthy level of rigour and business focus. The value of a brand is enormous, and therefore brands need to be managed. The value of corporate knowledge is also enormous, so why should that value not also be managed? Brand, reputation, knowledge, customer base, etc., are intangible assets with great value to the organisation, and to leave these assets unmanaged would seem to be foolish in the extreme!

However, the terminology you use is less important than the approach you take. If people don't like the term 'knowledge management', then you can avoid using the term initially. However, there is no need to be apologetic about applying the term 'management' to knowledge, and the term 'knowledge management' is a useful reminder, when knowledge sharing has proven its value, that knowledge needs to be captured, shared and applied with a degree of managed rigour.

2

Knowledge management models for services, operations and manufacturing

Many of the existing models for knowledge management were developed in a project environment. The well-known 'learn before, during and after' model, for example, presupposes activity that has a beginning, a middle and an end, so therefore has a 'before', a 'during' and an 'after'. This is not true of continuous service work, operational work, production or manufacturing work. Where work is continuous, there is only a 'during'.

However, even continuous operational or service activity has a measuring and reporting cycle, and it is this cycle, which I use as the basis for the model shown below.

This model has three main components. The base is a do/review cycle. This assumes that an operation or production unit will regularly measure its performance, and benchmark this against other operations within the company (or if it is the sole operation, that it will benchmark against past performance). Knowledge management links into this cycle in four ways:

1. The operation or production unit will learn during the 'do' phase by reviewing its own activity (perhaps using

Figure 2.1 **Knowledge management model for services, operations and manufacturing**

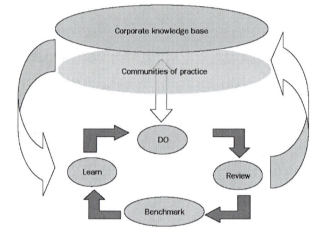

techniques such as the after action review, as described in Chapter 4) and by tapping in to the knowledge of the community, and the corporate knowledge base.

2. The operation or production unit will learn from the success of it's own performance during the review stage (perhaps using techniques such as the performance learning review (PLR), as described in Chapter 4).

3. The operation or production unit will benchmark itself against others, as described in Chapter 3, and will identify opportunities to learn and improve.

4. Finally the operation or production unit will learn from others. Techniques such as peer assist, site knowledge visit and knowledge exchange may be used, as described in Chapter 5, and a knowledge management plan may be developed, to co-ordinate this learning activity, as described in Chapter 10.

Some of the knowledge management activities associated with this cycle are shown below in Figure 2.2.

Figure 2.2   **Knowledge management activities**

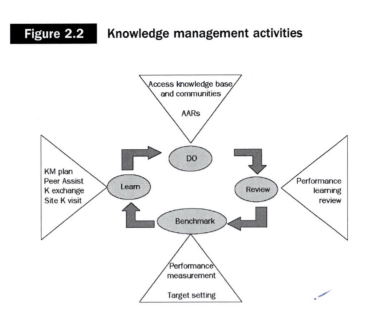

In addition to the activity cycle, the model includes two other elements:

1. the explicit corporate knowledge base, held in standards, operating procedures and best practices, and

2. the communities of practice, which hold the tacit knowledge base, and play a role in the ownership and transfer of knowledge as described in Chapter 6.

3

Performance benchmarking and knowledge management

Performance measurement, benchmarking, target setting and knowledge management are closely linked in an operation, production or manufacturing environment:

- performance measurement allows an operation or production unit to track its performance levels

- benchmarking allows it to compare those levels with other units, and identify the areas where it needs to improve, or areas where it can help others improve

- target setting allows it to focus on areas for improvement

- knowledge management allows it to acquire or develop the knowledge it needs in order to improve.

If you can measure and benchmark the performance of the same operation across different locations, you can identify the better performers and the poorer performance. For example, Figure 3.2 shows the cost performance for operations teams in six different locations. High costs equate to poor performance.

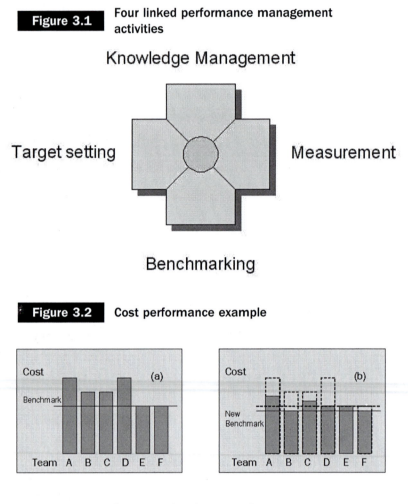

Figure 3.1 Four linked performance management activities

Knowledge Management

Target setting   Measurement

Benchmarking

Figure 3.2 Cost performance example

Teams E and F are the best performers, operating at benchmark costs, and A and D are the worst. These benchmarking data allow teams A and D to realise they have room for improvement, and allows them to set improvement targets. If all of these locations exchange knowledge, and the poorer performers learn from the better performers, then the overall performance should improve, as shown in Figure 3.2(b). All the teams except E have improved, and B and F have set a new benchmark.

Considerable costs have been cut out of the system.

What frequently happens is that the better performers find that even they have things to learn, and the collective benchmark performance often improves. The cost improvement shown in Figure 3.2(b), over all six teams, is 22%.

Internal benchmarking can therefore be a powerful means of measuring the potential value of knowledge management, and of identifying the knowledge suppliers and the knowledge users (in Figure 3.2a, teams E and F are primarily knowledge suppliers and teams A–D are knowledge users, though to an extent all locations both supply and use knowledge).

However, performance management and benchmarking are not always straightforward. If you are not clear on your performance metrics, you can't set a current benchmark nor establish a desired goal. For example, if you are a lawyer and you are drafting a confidentiality agreement for your client, how do you measure the success of your work? Is it successful if it is done quickly? Done cheaply? Done well? And who defines whether it is done well? How can you tell if one confidentiality agreement is better than another, and therefore which one is best practice?

When creating a benchmark system care must be taken to normalise the measurement across plants or locations. For example, if an activity takes 40 minutes at one plant and 65 minutes at another, are you sure you are comparing 'apples with apples'. Do you understand the context behind the measure? You should try to avoid having blind faith in a measure until you have assurance that the process to produce the measures is compatible, and that the data can be normalised for background conditions. In the example in Figure 3.2, the measures might have been comparing the cost to produce the same item, but perhaps team A uses batch production while team E uses continuous production. The technology being used in the different plants may also have an impact on the measure. However, even if the performance measures are robust, you will often hear units saying, 'but our situation is different. You cannot compare our costs with those of other units'. Sometimes this is valid, and sometimes this is an automatic reaction, which needs to be challenged.

One way to consider internal benchmarking is the development of a simple self-assessment tool. The purpose of self-assessment is to understand where and how you need to improve. The challenge is then to address the improvement opportunities in a systematic way. Once you have your data you then need to learn where you can improve, i.e. your largest gaps or quick wins and planning the closure of these priority gaps.

The main advantages of an assessment tool such as this is that it provides a starting point against which to measure future improvement and enables comparison with other parts of your organisation or businesses within the company. However, it is easy to become distracted and to focus on scores rather than improvement. Be prepared to manage unrealistic expectations. Remember the real point of using a value process is to improve performance.

Target setting

Once an operational or production unit has established its current performance level, and determined how it benchmarks against other units, then they (or their management) need to set targets for improvement.

Targets need to be achievable. The target will generally be set lower than the performance level already achieved elsewhere. In the example in Figure 3.2, team D would probably not set itself the target of exceeding the performance of team F, but might aim to get halfway towards team F's cost though applying learning from team F.

For example, an international production company recently benchmarked its water usage at plants around the world, and found a huge variation in performance. Instead of insisting that all plants should seek to perform at the level of the best, they measured the top quartile performance, and set a target for the lower performing plants of closing the gap to top quartile by 10%, through learning from the high performers. Even this apparently easy target would save them many millions of dollars annually.

What knowledge

One of the fundamental steps in knowledge management is to define what the key knowledge is, that needs to be managed. This is linked with the question of what are the key performance metrics that need to be measured.

Generally, the key performance areas for a company help define the key knowledge that needs to be managed. Ask yourself, in the context of the business strategy:

- What are the key things I need to do (and to perform well at), in order to deliver the strategy? Then ask

- What are the key things I need to know how to do, in order to do these things well?

However, not all key areas of knowledge need to be managed in the same way. Figure 3.3 shows a framework for deciding how to manage your key knowledge areas.

Figure 3.3 Categorisation of types of knowledge at company level

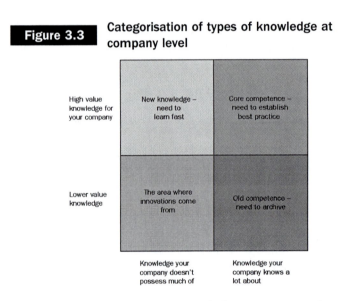

You can start to divide knowledge topics into four areas if you look at two components; the level of in-house knowledge that currently exists, and the level of in-house need for that knowledge. The horizontal axis of this diagram measures the level of in-house knowledge, i.e. how much does your organisation already know about this topic? The vertical axis of this diagram measures how important the knowledge is to your business, i.e. how much do you need to know?

- Where there is a high business need for the knowledge, but the level of in-house knowledge is not yet very high, then there is a need to learn, and the company will often set up learning programmes or task forces to acquire the knowledge. This is the area of new knowledge.

- Where there is a high business need for the knowledge, and the level of in-house knowledge is high, then you are looking at areas of core competence, and your focus should be on development and implementation of best practice and standards. This is the area where operational and production metrics need to be set (as described in the previous chapter) so that best practices can be identified, and turned into standards.

- Where there is a low business need for the knowledge, and the level of in-house knowledge is high, then you are looking at areas of old knowledge, and your focus should be on archiving this knowledge in case it's needed again in future, or even on out-sourcing it.

- Where there is a low business need for the knowledge, and the level of in-house knowledge is also low, then you might consider that this is not an area of interest at all in terms of knowledge management. However, it is often from this area that the new innovations arise, and areas of new technology are generated, which need to be pushed up into the 'learn rapidly' box.

- Any one operational or production unit will also identify core knowledge, which it needs to manage. Generally the core knowledge areas are set by the corporation, and measured (as described above) through performance metrics and compared through benchmarking. For any one operational or production unit, the individual performance metrics can be plotted on a matrix such as that shown in Figure 3.4, which will help define the knowledge management plan for the unit.

- Where the benchmarking shows that the unit is performing at a higher level than the company as a whole, then the unit needs to concentrate on sharing knowledge with the rest of the organisation, in order to improve overall performance. Benchmarking data will also help it target individual units that most need help.

- Where the benchmarking shows that the unit is performing at a lower level than the company as a whole,

Figure 3.4 Categorisation of types of knowledge at unit level

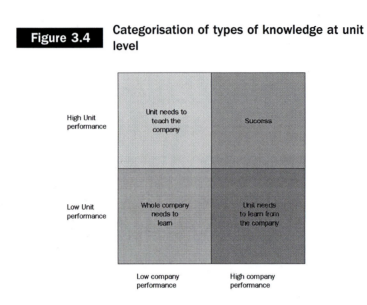

then the unit needs to concentrate on acquiring knowledge from the rest of the organisation, in order to improve unit performance. Benchmarking data will help identify individual units to learn from.

- Where the benchmarking shows that the unit and the organisation are performing at a low level, then the organisation as a whole needs to acquire knowledge. Topics that fall in to this box will also fall into the top left box in Figure 3.4.

- Where the benchmarking shows that the unit and the organisation are performing at a high level, then the organisation is doing well. Knowledge topics falling in this area will not be the focus of knowledge management plans for individual units.

4

Processes for learning from performance

In this chapter I will review some of the processes that can be used in an operational and manufacturing environment for learning from performance. These include:

- After action review (AAR)
- Performance learning review (PLR).

After action review

In operational and manufacturing environments the AAR process is well suited to reviewing learning from performance. They are simple to conduct and have immediate benefit. They can be used at many scales. For example, AAR have been used in many manufacturing plants and call centres at shift handover time to capture what was learned during the previous shift.

AARs are applied in many industries as a mechanism for learning during project activity. They are focused review meetings, relatively short in duration, designed to help the team become conscious of their own knowledge, so they can act on that knowledge as work progresses. It is like 'learning on Tuesday to perform better on Wednesday'. In addition, the learning can be transferred to other teams, but this is generally a secondary role.

The AAR process was developed by the US Army, who use it as their main knowledge-gathering process. As described here, it does not go into very great analytical depth, and so is useful for reviewing short-turnaround activity, or single actions. It is short and focused enough to do on a weekly or daily basis, perhaps at the end of a production run. For example, a refining company might use AARs after each shift during maintenance activity. A production unit might use an AAR every week, or every month as monthly figures are published.

The structure of an AAR is very simple. It consists of asking four questions. The questions are answered through dialogue within the team.

1. **What was supposed to happen?** The first question is asked about the objective of the activity, and the target performance. In an operational and manufacturing environment it should talk about the production target to be achieved during the period under consideration.

2. **What actually happened?** The second question looks at actual performance. If you are conducting an AAR, you need to establish 'ground truth' with this question. You are looking to determine reality, rather than opinion. This is where the measurement system and 'facts' about what was actually achieved are discussed.

3. **Why was there a difference?** The third question seeks to understand why a particular result was achieved. Perhaps you did better than expected; perhaps you did worse than expected. Perhaps you delivered more than, or less than, the operational target. What were the factors that determined the result? For brevity, this is frequently

noted on the flip chart as 3 up, 3 down (see Figure 4.1). Another way to ask this question, if the first way doesn't work, is **'What went well, and what did not go so well?'**

4. **What have we learned** (including actions arising)? The final question asks about the learning, and should be expressed in terms of what will be done differently the next day (or, in cases of overperformance, what should be repeated the next day). Here you move from analysis of the activity, to 'What are we going to do about it?'. Many times, actions for improvement will be identified, which should be entered into any company action tracking system.

The answers to these questions can usefully be recorded on a one-page pro forma (or a marked up flip chart – Figure 4.1), which can be collected for future reference.

Figure 4.1   Flip chart marked up for an AAR

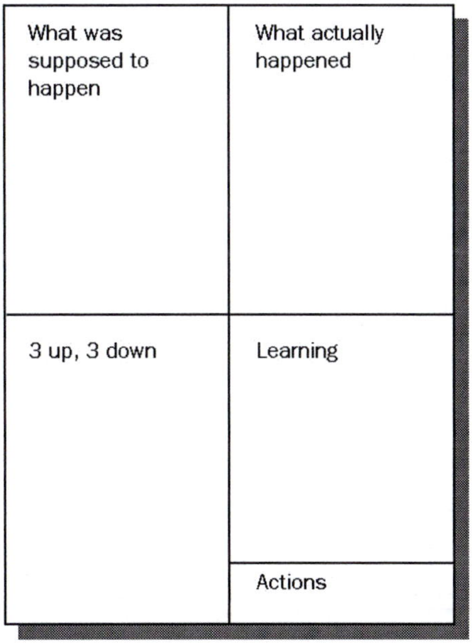

What was supposed to happen	What actually happened
3 up, 3 down	Learning
	Actions

The following example is from an AAR held at the end of a shift in a plant producing aluminium tubes, and shows the level of detail required during an AAR.

- **What was supposed to happen?** (1) produce 5000 metres of number 2 tube, (2) produce the tube as per specification, (3) no HSE incidents.

- **What actually happened?** (1) produced 5500 metres of number 2 tube, (2) 500 metres of tube damaged during storage operations, (3) potential damage to employee incident recorded during storage operations.

- **3 up, 3 down?** (1) New rollers at point 7 allowed the rig to be run at 5% above the speed specified in the procedure, (2) racks were set up for the expected production. Tubes were put on to racks that were full rather than starting a new stack, stack became overfull and toppled over.

- **What have we learned?** (1) The rollers at point 7 were replaced as per planned maintenance programme. New rollers allowed the rig to run at higher speed. (2) The current supply of racks is inadequate and poses a risk to operations and to safety.

- **Actions?** (1) Request engineering to evaluate cost balance of increased production verses reduced time between replacement of rollers. (2) Have additional racks readily available in case production exceeds anticipated levels.

Although the learning here is only about small things, having additional racks available, based on day-by-day routine learning, can give a massive performance improvement in the long run.

The AAR process works well in an open, blame-free, inclusive environment. You may need to set the ground rules for AARs, and some of the rules are as follows.

- Aim for openness, not hiding any mistakes
- There should be no hierarchy – everyone's input is equally valid
- The focus of the exercise is learning, not blame or evaluation
- Everyone who was involved in the activity should take part in the AAR
- No outsiders should be present, nobody should be there to 'audit performance'
- Deal with the significant issues and the significant objectives, not trivia.

Performance learning review

The PLR is used to gather learning from the whole annual cycle of production, manufacturing or operations. It reviews your performance against the annual target that was set after the last benchmarking cycle.

If benchmarking and target setting happens at a shorter time-scale than annually, e.g. quarterly benchmarking and target setting, then the review also needs to be at this shorter time-scale.

It is important to schedule the PLR at the end of the production or operational cycle, when the performance metrics have been gathered, and prior to the benchmarking, target setting and knowledge management planning exercises.

Somebody who was not part of the operational team should facilitate the review. Under no circumstances should the team self-facilitate; they definitely need somebody external, who can help steer the process, ask the awkward questions, and make sure any undiscussables are discussed. Find a good facilitator who has a clear idea of the review process, and of the purpose of the exercise. PLRs are not complicated meetings, but they do need attention to purpose and attention to behaviours. Understanding, and following, the process is key to a successful outcome.

The meeting will take at least half a day, more usually a day, and should be attended by the extended operations team and their manager. Anyone who had an influence on performance should attend, down to a level of shift supervisors, or even operators.

The flow of the review meeting is similar to that of the AAR, in being focused on the measurable difference between the assessment position and the current position. However, it goes into far greater depth than the AAR.

The process covers:

- An introduction to the process
- The performance targets set at the beginning of the year (or other production cycle)
- The results achieved
- The root causes behind any areas of overperformance or successful performance in each performance area, and the learnings and actions that arise from these
- The root causes behind any areas of underperformance or unsuccessful performance, and the learnings and actions that arise from these
- Any procedures and standards that need to be updated and who will action them?

Let's look at each of these steps in a bit more detail. Some examples are included as illustrations.

- *Introduction.* The first step in a review is to set the scene by discussing the purpose of the meeting, the process of the meeting, and the ground rules for the meeting. Make it clear that the meeting is held to capture the learnings, in order to help future performance. The purpose of the meeting is not to assign blame or to assign praise, but to make life easier for the next operational cycle. Also make it clear what you will do with the output from the meeting, especially if you are recording the event. Once PLRs have become an established standard process, you don't really need to set the scene, but where this is a new process then you may need some careful set-up at the beginning of the meeting.

- *Targets*
  - *Example* – reduce the current material wastage on line 5 from 7% to 4% of total throughput

This should refer back to the benchmark exercise at the beginning of the year and the targets set for the year. The actual reports or records of these events should be tabled and agreement sought from all present that this is what you set out to achieve. If for any reason you find there is disagreement on what you set out to achieve (perhaps there were hidden objectives, or a lack of clarity) spend whatever time is necessary to resolve this disagreement and don't proceed until everyone is in agreement that 'this is what we set out to achieve'

- *Results*
  - *Example* – material wastage on line 5 is currently at 3.7% per annum, so the target has been met, and exceeded.

Ensure you base this discussion on the metrics that you have compiled during the year and which you will be reporting.

- *The root causes behind any areas of overperformance or successful performance, and the learnings that arise from these*

  - *Example* – we held discussions with line 3, which has the lowest material wastage. It is a different process and different materials but we learned that they keep the material in sealed containers until just before it is required.

  - Preheating the material seems to be one of the key means of managing waste in line 5. We tried 65°C and got good results. We are currently using 72°C but think this might not be the optimum setting.

  This stage of the meeting is about identifying what worked well but perhaps more importantly, why it worked well. Gentle probing might be required to get to a full and complete understanding of why and how it might be repeated. In the example above you might want to continue probing to understand temperature ramp up times or how long the material is held at that temperature prior to it being used. You want to continue until you understand the root causes in enough detail that you could replicate this success on other lines or in other plants.

- *The root causes behind any areas of underperformance or disappointing performance, and the learnings and actions that arise from these*

  - *Example* – we tried decreasing the speed of the process to see if it would result in less wastage. This resulted in reduced throughput of product with little impact on wastage

- The analogue gauges were replaced with digital ones and while they are easier for the operators to read it made no measurable difference to the wastage reduction challenge.

Be careful with the use of language at this stage. Use neutral words such as 'disappointing' rather than negative words such as 'wrong'. You should assume that people were trying their best to achieve the targets set. You need to be very careful that you don't allow any sense of blame to enter into the discussion. You want to focus on learning why the target wasn't achieved and what you would do differently next time.

- *What procedures and standards need to be updated and who will action them?*
  - *Example* – update the procedure to keep the material sealed in containers until it is actually needed and preheat the material. Ramp the temperature up at 1°C per minute until it reaches 75°C and hold it there for 30 minutes.

If you find as a result of the PLR meeting that procedures and standards need to be updated this is the point in the meeting that accountability for doing this is allocated. Include a feedback or reporting loop that informs everyone that the updates have been done and that the documents have been updated as a result of learning from within the organisation. This later step reinforces that learning is important in the organisation and that things change as a result of it.

The output from the review session should be packaged and communicated to those team members who weren't able to attend.

Occasionally, when reviewing a challenging operational

cycle, conflict may arise. Different people at the PLR may have different perceptions of what happened to cause poor performance. Arguments can start, tempers can rise. The way to turn conflict into a positive outcome is to ask the question 'What should we do *next year (or in other plants)*, to ensure this breakdown or failure does not happen again?'. In many ways it does not matter precisely what happened this time, or whose fault it was, so long as everybody is agreed on how to do it better next time. In fact, the question 'What should we do next time' is the most powerful question to ask in a PLR.

5

Processes for learning from others

In this chapter I will review some of the processes that can be used in an operational and manufacturing environment for learning from other operation and manufacturing units. These include:

- Peer assist

- Site knowledge visit

- Knowledge exchange

- Business driven action learning.

Peer assist

During the benchmarking process, you may identify a number of other operational, service, production or manufacturing units who are performing better than you in one key area of performance. A peer assist is a means of learning from these other units, through inviting them to visit and share their knowledge with you.

- A peer assist is a meeting where the operational unit invites people with relevant knowledge and experience, to come and share it with them. Peer assists are one of the simplest and most effective ways of bringing tacit knowledge into an operational unit, they are so effective that the management of many organisations are making them an expectation of how an operational unit will operate their business. The success of peer assists depends on the following factors:

- *The peer assist needs clear objectives.* The peers are bringing their knowledge to the operational unit for a purpose, namely to help increase your performance in the identified area. Try and define some deliverables linked to that performance area. Sample deliverables might be 'provide options to decrease our production cost by 5%'

- *The peer assist should be focused on 'assisting'.* In other words, it is a meeting where the operational unit needs help and assistance, which is provided by the visiting peers. The unit therefore needs to be open to learning, and their peers need to be willing to share their knowledge and experience. If the meeting falls into 'attack and defend' behaviours, then it has failed its purpose. Good facilitation will avoid this happening.

- *The peer assist should truly involve peers*, i.e. the peers of the operational team. These are not meetings where you bring in experts or senior managers. Bring in people at the same operational level who have experience to share. People are far more open to learning from, and sharing with, their peers, and this removes all the politics associated with management hierarchies.

The ideal structure for a peer assist is a four-part structure.

- In the first part of the meeting, after the introductions and welcome, the operational team explains their context, their last year's performance, their target for improvement, and any constraints they may be working under.

- In the second part of the meeting, the peers discuss their knowledge and experience from their own operating units.

- In the third part of the meeting, the host unit and the visiting peers go though a process of dialogue, often in small groups, as they attempt to use past experience to improve the operational unit's performance.

- In the final part of the meeting, the visiting peers confer, then feed back their recommendations to the host operational team.

As an example peer assist, one company supplying bottled gas wished to better understand how to track the cylinders that it was supplying to customers. Their target was to reduce 'mislaid' cylinders by 14%. In addition to learning from within its own organisation they invited non-competitors who had experience in logistics to participate in the peer assist. By having the external view included they were not only able to learn from experience from within their own organisation but were additionally able to learn from other industries. At the end of the peer assist not only did they feel confident that they would be able to meet their target when the ideas created in the peer assist were implemented, but also each of the visitors went away with insights as to how they too could improve their own logistic processes.

Another company held a peer assist on pipe inspection. On almost any industrial plant you will find pipe work with flanged joints and while the aspiration is to have zero leakage, leakage does happen. Pipe inspection is an ongoing maintenance activity. The company in question had 4.8% of joints failing leak tests and wished to be able to achieve a target failure rate of less than 1% within 2 years. A peer assist was held to which engineers and technicians with relevant experience from other plants were invited. As a result of the meeting a formal training course was developed for operators making up pipe joints, standard bolt lubricant and load calculations were developed for all plant locations. The achieved result was under 0.5% with an associated reduction in system re-tests from just over 30% to under 5%.

Site knowledge visit

Tell me and I know
Show me and I understand
Let me do it and I'll remember it forever

The above saying is the foundation and justification for knowledge visits.

When the benchmarking process has indicated a need to close a knowledge and performance gap, and also identified a group who clearly hold the knowledge as evidenced by their performance results, then a site knowledge visit is another method that can be used to access that knowledge. A selection of people from the operating unit can visit the high-performing unit at their place of work, ask them questions, see them in action, try things out for themselves, and go back to their unit with a new level of operational knowledge. The site knowledge visit is focused on the visitors obtaining knowledge that they can take back to their location, and is different from other site visits such as a review, audit, inspection or due diligence visit. The visit will generally have three stages:

- Set-up
- Knowledge transfer
- Debrief.

The relative lengths of the three components can vary significantly. A site knowledge visit can be a 1-day Q&A session with a team of visitors, or it could involve one operator working at another site for a period of weeks to learn some of the local techniques. In the early stages of Ford's knowledge management programme, they instigated a whole series of operator site visits as a means of exchanging knowledge.

A site knowledge visit is not a 'show and tell' event but rather a process whereby one group outlines the knowledge it wishes to obtain, it then works with the group who have that knowledge, they then take that knowledge back to their own workplace and implement it there.

Setting up the site knowledge visit (positioning, briefing)

A site knowledge visit may be a new concept, both for the hosts and the visitors. They will be used to 'tourist' visits, and it will be easy for them to fall into familiar roles of 'tourist guide' and 'passive observers'. But what you really want is an on-site process of dialogue around the key issues, and it is worth setting things up so that both sides are well prepared.

Position the visit carefully

A site knowledge visit can be disruptive. A number of key staff may have to take time out from their daily operations in order to host the visiting team. They may be resentful of this, they may not see the point, they may imagine it is another tourist visit, or another bunch of managers wanting a walkabout. You need to position the visit very carefully. Key to this is securing high-level support; someone who can position the visit as being critical for the business. Get them to send out a note setting the context for the visit such as the example below.

To: B McGrew, Site Manager, Fire Response Coordination Centre, Trumpington

Site Knowledge Visit

Dear Barney

When we conducted the annual performance management and benchmarking cycle in the Chigley Fire Service last month, we identified Vehicle Incident Response as an area of focus for improvement. We are very well aware of your excellent record in this field, and would very much like to learn from you.

I have asked Charlie Foxtrot from the knowledge management team to set up a site knowledge visit for key members of the Fire Response Centre teams. Charlie will be in touch with you shortly to arrange an itinerary for the visit, and I would be very grateful if you could give him every support and assistance. The purpose of the visit is for you to help the visitors learn as much as possible about effective Vehicle Incident response.

In addition, Charlie and his team will take detailed notes from the visit, in order to start to document some of the best practices you are using.

Thank you in advance for your help in this matter.

Regards,

Albert Pugh, Manager, Chigley Fire Brigade

Another thing you may wish to consider is to get one of the visiting team to phone the location that they wish to visit and explain how important this is to them. Explain that this is not just a routine tourist-type visit, but a bunch of guys who really want to understand how things are done at that location in order to improve their own operation. They want to find out the detail, the hints and tips to allow them to replicate the success at their location.

Select who should go

The people who should go on the site visit are people who will use the knowledge. For example, a site knowledge visit looking at facilities management issues should be attended by facilities managers. A site knowledge visit looking at production line methods should be attended by production line foremen and supervisors. These people will want to talk with their peers at the site, see their local issues and solutions, and even work with them for a while.

Brief the visitors about their role

The visiting team at a site visit must realise that they are not there as passive observers, but have an active role. Their responsibility is to learn as much as they can. They have a questioning role. They must ask as many questions as they need in order to be able to carry the learning away with them. They need to be alert and curious, and take detailed notes. Their role is almost that of a spy, but a spy in friendly territory. They may have the opportunity to try our some of the equipment, or even to work with the home team for a while. Make sure they realise that the point of this is not necessarily to do a good job, but to learn as much as possible. Prepare a briefing note for them so they understand their role (see the example below). Discuss with them the level of detail required in their note-taking required. An example briefing note is shown below.

Dear Team

Over the next 2 days we will be visiting Trumpington Fire Response Coordination Centre to learn about how to improve our Vehicle Incident response.

The aim of this visit is to allow us to see first hand what good practice Vehicle Incident Response looks and feels like in operation, and for you to pick up as much valuable and practical knowledge as possible, to help us improve our own performance in this area. Remember also that you are there as a representative from your operation, and your colleagues will be eager to apply the learnings you gather. Make sure you capture enough detail that you can teach them on your return.

In previous site knowledge visits I have found it useful for participants to be asking themselves questions during such visits. So, for example during the next 2 days you might wish to ask yourself:

- What have I seen that works really well?
- Why is it working so well?
- How can I replicate this in my operation?
- What are the pitfalls and risks concerning effective Vehicle Incident Response that I wasn't aware of before?
- How can I avoid these in my own operation?
- What are the issues which have been raised, which still need answering?

As you listen to the various people that we meet on the visit, keep asking yourself 'Have I understood this sufficiently well that I could now go and do it myself?'. If you need more detail, ask for it. If they say for example 'Allow yourself sufficient time to do this task'; ask 'How much is sufficient?'. If they say 'we had terrible problems with this part of the operation' ask them 'If you were doing it all over again, how would you avoid those problems?'. Always ensure you have the level of detail and sequence that you need to be able to repeat it when you get back home.

This may be your only chance to learn from Trumpington. You may never come back here, so make sure you collect and take away all the knowledge you and your colleagues will need.

Regards,

Albert Pugh, Manager, Chigley Fire Brigade

Prepare the host team for their role

The role of the host team is to be as open and generous as possible with their knowledge. Because the visiting team are there to learn, not judge or review, there is no benefit in hiding anything from them. If disclosure is an issue, it is quite possible to make a deal that some things can be said 'off the record', and the home team can ask for editorial rights on any visit notes or knowledge asset. The host team should see themselves as teachers, and can consider ways in which they can demonstrate their knowledge in action. Could the visitors try out some tasks, or machinery? Can the host team simulate a special event or an emergency, for the visitors to watch? It will be valuable to demonstrate 'business as usual', or the plant operating under ideal conditions, but would it be good to show the visitors what you do if things go wrong? The host team should also make sure that anyone with specialist knowledge is available for the site visit.

Site visit agenda

The host team should present the context, and the key learnings

Have a presentation and questions session before any walk-about or hands-on session. Make sure you have the expertise in the room to answer almost any question the visiting team will ask. The host team can explain the context of the site, their challenges, their solutions, and a general breakdown of how they operate. You need this to give context to any more practical session. Allow the visitors to question as deeply as they need to. Inevitably many answers will be 'we will see this as we walk around the site' – but that is OK, as it means the visitors will know what to look out for. If the host team use slides to structure the presentation, make sure these are available to the visitors as handouts.

In a recent site visit, the presentation (which might have taken half an hour to stand up and deliver without questions) took between 2½ and 3 hours because it became a general discussion round about the presentation. The host manager would put up the slide and say something, one of the visitors would ask a question, and one of the other experts would answer it. It went very well. Having the slides gave the meeting structure, to make sure that we covered the key points of what they had learned at the site.

Spend time looking at the reality of operations

One of the main purposes of going to visit the host team, is to see them in operation. Have a walk around the site, look at the way people are working, look at the systems and procedures in place, look at the equipment, the building, the roles and skills of the staff. The visitors should be prepared to question as deeply as they need to. Allow the visitors to try things out, as much as safety and operations will allow. Let them 'steer the ship' for a bit! This could be as brief as trying out a control interface for part of a shift, or as complex as trying a simulated emergency. Alternatively, if time allows, one or more of the visitors could spend a day or a week working alongside the host team, to really understand the way they operate. It is probably better if one of the experts or local operators takes you on the walk around rather than the manager, because they really know the detail of the building or the site. The manager does not have that much detail.

Arrange a summary and debrief

The manager of the host team will no doubt want to give a summary of the visit, and this can be couched around 'What are the key learnings I would like you to take away?'. However, it is even more powerful to ask the visiting team to spend half an hour together to prepare a presentation on 'what we have learned'. As they build this presentation they will share their learnings with each other, and by articulating their learnings they will remember them better. As they feed the learnings back to the host team, the host team can add additional context, and correct them if they have got their details wrong.

Record the site knowledge visit

Only a small number of people will be able to go on a site knowledge visit, but there will be many more people who need to share in the knowledge. The visitors will need to share what they have learned with their colleagues when they get back, for example. There will be people who could not make the visit, due to scheduling difficulties, but who still need the knowledge. And there will almost certainly be others in future who are involved in similar activities. Use the site knowledge visit as an opportunity to build a knowledge asset, for future reference.

Make sure the visitors take detailed notes

The most basic form of recording is for the visitors to take detailed notes. Provide them with clip boards or notebooks, and plenty of pencils and pens. Encourage them to make the notes as detailed as possible. Encourage them to record the questions asked, as well as the answers.

Record the presentations and discussions on audio or video

The best way to transfer knowledge in your knowledge asset, is in the words of the people involved. When you come to construct the asset, then you need access to verbatim quotes and stories, and a transcript of the meeting will be the raw material you use. There is no real substitute for audio recording, though speed-writing or touch typing may also give a reasonably good result. If you are going to audio-record the meeting, you need to think carefully about the equipment you use. Placing a cassette recorder in the middle of the room, using the recorders inbuilt microphone, will not work. The recording will be dominated by motor noise, and people furthest away will be inaudible. Invest in some table microphones, with adapters to feed them into the recorder, and use a lapel microphone for the presenter. Appoint someone to watch the recorder. Someone else needs to make fairly detailed notes of who said what, so the quotes and recommendations can be attributed. Also these detailed notes are a back-up in case of equipment failure.

Take a video camera on the walk-around or hands-on session

The objective here is not to record the entire site visit, but to have tape available for extracting still photographs, or video clips of key techniques or important features. It is far better to take a recording and never use it, than it is to need it and not have it. Concentrate on recording those aspects that need to be transferred visually. If you can't get hold of a video camera, take still photographs. Make sure you photograph anyone who contributed to the knowledge asset, or who could be a contact for knowledge in the future.

For example, in BP, benchmarking showed that Castellon refinery was a high performer in many of the production metrics. So as part of a site visit, a camera crew were invited to make a film of the operators at Castellon telling the story of how they had achieved their high performance, which could be shared with other production units around the company.

Have a clear idea of the final outcome before you start recording

The main written outcome from the sit visit is a knowledge asset. This needs to contain:

- guidelines for the future
- history from the project to illustrate the guidelines
- names and contact details of the people involved, for future reference, and
- any key artefacts, including photographs.

So this determines what you need to record from the site visit (the fall-back being, of course, to record everything). Record as accurately as possible what the lessons and recommendations are for the future.

Make sure you circulate the write-up around the participants for editorial comment

Make sure nobody was misquoted, and that your wording of the lessons really reflects the views of the team. Give people a chance to reword what they said. Many people are free and open in speech, but wish to be more guarded in print. Make sure everyone realises that their quotes will be attributed. They will not be anonymous.

Feed back what you have learned

Once the visit is over, you need to share the learning. This need not be in the form of a report. One company took two plant managers from Romania to visit another operation in South Africa, and they took video cameras with them. When they got back to Romania they said they didn't want to write a report, they wanted to go around the Romanian operational sites and do a visual presentation of what they had seen in South Africa. About 50 people attended at each site, and everybody could see what they were talking about on the screen.

Knowledge exchange

The knowledge exchange is a process for many operational units to exchange knowledge and experience in one area of performance. It is normally used in situations where an improvement target has been established for several locations or operating units and they wish to learn together. The BBC case study in Chapter 12 describes knowledge exchanges used by the Sport Department and the Nations and regions, while the CfBT case study (Chapter 12) describes knowledge exchange symposiums.

A knowledge exchange is the term I use for a meeting where people from several locations come together to share knowledge with several knowledge customers. Several teams provide knowledge, several teams require knowledge. These can be very high-powered creative meetings, often pivotal in the development of an organisation's knowledge. A knowledge exchange can be thought of as a situation where several groups each have a piece of the knowledge and they have come together to share and combine their respective knowledge for the benefit of all.

The structure of the exchange might contain the following elements:

- identification of key issues
- dialogue around the issues
- validation of shared knowledge
- feedback.

A tremendous amount of knowledge is generated at a knowledge exchange. This knowledge needs to be captured, and will form the basis for a knowledge asset. Recording the knowledge exchange is important, and needs to be given attention. The knowledge exchange can often double as a kick-off meeting for a community of practice, with the invitees forming the core of the community. The knowledge exchange process has four stages:

- setting up the knowledge exchange (who to invite, choosing a location)
- the knowledge exchange – format (deciding the issues, assigning the groups)
- recording the knowledge exchange
- follow-up to the knowledge exchange (building the community of practice, publishing the knowledge asset).

Setting up the knowledge exchange

A knowledge exchange is a very intensive programme of knowledge sharing, packed into a small time span. It is worth giving careful thought to setting it up, to make sure it goes smoothly.

Assign an organisation team

A knowledge exchange can be quite a large event, and needs at least two people, possibly more, to form an organisation team. People are needed to fill the following roles (although some members of the team could hold more than one of these roles):

- A **business sponsor** for the event, to provide funding and business context. Someone sufficiently high level to give legitimacy to the event.
- An **organiser**, to act as project manager for the knowledge exchange.
- One or more **facilitators**.

- Someone to handle **logistics** (travel, accommodation, etc.).
- Someone to co-ordinate **recording** the event.
- Someone to **package the knowledge** afterwards.

Some of the more specialised aspects of the knowledge exchange, such as facilitation, recording and knowledge packaging, can be outsourced, and for a really big event, you may want to hire a conference organiser.

Decide scope and objectives

You have to be clear on the topic to be covered at the knowledge exchange. If the scope is not well defined, the event can expand out of control. The best sort of knowledge to address in a knowledge exchange is an area that is being developed simultaneously in several areas of the company, where knowledge is not yet codified and standardised, and where there is great business benefit from consolidating what the company knows. For example, BP held a knowledge exchange on 'knowledge management' at an early stage in their knowledge management initiative, to develop a common understanding of practices, processes and options.

Choose a location

Choose an offsite location somewhere quiet. Don't try and hold a knowledge exchange at the office – people will be distracted, and you will lose the opportunities for socialisation, which will be important in building the community spirit. Use a conference hotel, with onsite catering, and book a main room and several smaller rooms for group work sessions. Choose somewhere that has easy access – either with rail and motorway access (if everyone is in the same country), or with an international hub airport (for international travellers).

Decide who to invite

Invite a group of experienced people who are involved in the topic area. These may be people with experience to share, but you can also invite people starting work in this topic area who want access to the knowledge. Everyone invited to the event will be a potential knowledge customer, and many of the people will also be knowledge suppliers. Choose people from a wide geographical spread – preferably one or more people from each business unit involved in the topic. For example, a company recently held a knowledge exchange on 'public service contracts', and invited people from several such contracts in the UK, plus others who were bidding for similar contracts in the USA and Asia-Pacific. Aim for between 15 and 40 people; 20–30 is a good number. Select people who are pretty much peers. Don't invite senior managers; they may inhibit open discussion.

Send out an invitation letter

Give the invitees a few weeks notice, and send out an invitation letter. Ideally this letter should come from the business sponsor. One of the biggest risks to the success of a knowledge exchange is failing to attract the right people, and the best way around this is to use a 'big name' to invite people. If the sponsor has a 'message' for the exchange (or a request, or a challenge for the participants), then get this message at least a month in advance, before the agenda is finalised. An example invitation letter is shown below.

To: (invitation list)

Invitation to the 'Managing Subcontractors' knowledge exchange.

Thank you for agreeing to attend the knowledge exchange workshop on 'What Cubco knows about Managing Subcontractors, which is being held at the Townhall Hotel on the 13 and 14 November 2007.

As you know, our recent expansion over the last year has led to an increased use by several of our business units of subcontractors. Similar growth in the use of subcontractors is forecast for the next year or so. If we get the use of subcontracts right, we will be well on track to delivering our growth agenda in the new markets. If, on the other hand, we fail to learn the lessons of this year, then we will not deliver the performance we have promised the analysts. This knowledge exchange is crucial to developing the knowledge base which will underpin our future success.

Within the next week, you will be contacted by Julie Delta of the knowledge management team, to talk through your contribution to this event, your knowledge needs, and the knowledge you will bring. Logistics for the event will be co-ordinated by Tim Lewis.

The knowledge exchange will start at 0900 on the 13 November, and the second day will finish at approximately 1800. An agenda is attached. A dinner has been arranged for all delegates on the Monday evening, commencing with pre-dinner drinks in the

Terrace Lounge at approximately 1930. Could you let Tim know by 1400 on Friday 10 November if you will require a vegetarian meal. The dress code for the workshop will be smart casual (e.g. ties and jackets not necessary). Please find attached directions to the hotel. Do not hesitate to contact Julie or Tim should you have any questions.

Regards,

Windy Miller, Managing Director, Camberwick Green Millers

Speak to the attendees beforehand

It is well worth a phone call to each of the participants before the event, to ask the following questions:

- What knowledge will you bring to this exchange? What are the areas within the identified topic where you feel you have a lot of knowledge and experience to offer? These need not be areas where your business has performed well – you may have learned the hard way!
- What knowledge will you take away from this exchange? What are the areas where you feel you have a lot to learn?
- What would make this exchange a success for your business unit?
- What are your concerns about the exchange?

It can be useful to make up a table of 'knowledge needs and knowledge offers' before the knowledge exchange, to begin the process of surfacing issues (see example below). Why not set up a 'knowledge exchange website', with details of location, agenda, participants, etc., and post this table for people to look at.

Table 5.1	Knowledge needs and knowledge offers. What Camberwick Green Millers knows about managing subcontractors: gives and takes

Each of the four regional offices has proposed areas where it has knowledge to offer others, and areas where it needs to learn from others

What can others learn from Brussels? *Screening of potential candidates*	What can others learn from Chicago? *Building teams* *Business processes*	What can others learn from Japan? *Creating joint objectives*	What can others learn from Australia? *Creating delivery plans* *Inspection and QA/QC*
What can Brussels learn from others? *Managing end customer expectations*	What can Chicago learn from others? *Compliance auditing* *Quality assurance*	What can Japan learn from others? How to optimise payment schedules *Single and multiple sourcing*	What can Australia learn from others? *Teaching subcontractors our HSE standards*

Agenda

The knowledge exchange format is an exercise in organising dialogue between a large group of people. The best way to do this is to break up into smaller groups to discuss specific topics, and reconvene regularly for feedback and wider discussion. This pattern can be interspersed with group discussions, for variety (especially later in the exchange, when people are comfortable with the process).

State the purpose of the knowledge exchange, the objectives and the ground rules

It is good to kick off the formal part of the knowledge exchange with an explanation of why it has been called, what its objectives and deliverables are, why it is important to the business, how it will be conducted, what the purpose of the recording is, and what end product will be produced. Go through the agenda, discuss roles, make sure everyone understands what they are there to do.

But first, a word from our sponsor

It can be useful to start the knowledge exchange with an introduction from the business sponsor, describing the importance of the exchange, and the business need. If they cannot attend in person, then ask them to record a short video message, which can be shown at the start. Ensure that the message is not overwhelming but sets an achievable challenge.

Consider some presentations

If people are coming to the knowledge exchange with some crucial and relevant experiences, then consider giving them some time to present to the group. This will certainly be needed if you invite people from outside the company to share their knowledge. However, dialogue is a better mechanism for sharing knowledge than presentation, so keep the presentations short (e.g. 10 minutes) and follow them with Q&A sessions.

Decide the issues where knowledge needs to be exchanged

You need some way to divide up the entire topic under discussion, into meaningful chunks. There are a number of ways to do this:

- If you are exchanging knowledge about a business process, consider dividing the process into its component parts, as a flow chart or timeline.
- You could brainstorm, group, sort and rank the key issues.
- You could use the list of knowledge 'gives and takes' developed prior to the meeting. Allow the group to review this list, to add other issues if necessary.

Can you debate the issues as one large group?

Dialogue in one big group is possible, and some of the issues can be covered this way. You will get a more open dialogue in a smaller group, so whole-group sessions are more effective later in the exchange.

Otherwise, divide into smaller groups to dialogue

The meeting can be split into a number of smaller groups to discuss the list of issues or the components of the process. The smaller groups can discuss the same issue in parallel, or you can divide the meeting into separate groups to discuss separate issues. It really depends on how many issues you need to cover. Each issue will need a couple of hours dialogue, and 15–20 minutes feedback and discussion time. So, two or three issues could be discussed in a day by groups working the same issue in parallel, or eight to 12 issues by four groups working two or three issues each. Be certain about what you are asking the group to do. For example, you might say 'Discuss the main learnings around this issue, and what messages you would give to others based on your experience. Be prepared for one of your group to give a 10-minute flipchart-based summary of your learnings, back in the main room in 2 hours time'. For each group, somebody needs to be appointed as facilitator, and somebody needs to be appointed as recorder or 'scribe'.

Think carefully how you will divide the people into groups

You are aiming for diversity – don't put people with their friends, put them with people from other operational units. To an extent you can let people self-select which issue they would like to discuss, but keep an eye on the make-up of the groups. Consider remixing the groups on day 2.

Hold a dialogue around the issues

The dialogue session is where the bulk of the knowledge will come from. The facilitator needs to get this dialogue going, and steer it to delivering valuable output. However, most of the time the conversation takes off rapidly and barely pauses for breath. If conversation flags, the following questions may be useful:

- What have been the key success factors in this area?
- How was this success achieved?
- If you were doing it all over again, how would you approach it?
- What are the key challenges in this area?
- How have people tackled them?

- Is there anything you wish you had done (with the benefit of hindsight)?
- Any anecdotes or war stories?
- What would be your three, five or 10 pieces of advice for other sites?

Reconvene and feed back

The groups reconvene in the main room, and each group feeds back their findings for discussion in the wider group. The feedback sessions can usefully be recorded on audio or video. Also make sure you also record the details of the discussion that follows, as much valuable knowledge may be exchanged.

'How do we continue this exchange when the meeting is over'

The attendees at the knowledge exchange form a community of practice. If actions plans have been identified and agreed, then they might have formed the nucleus of a community of purpose. They will have developed some close relationships in the 2 or 3 days, and will have formed the basis of trust, respect and knowledge awareness that will form the foundation for future knowledge sharing. The attendees, now a nascent community, need to agree the processes for keeping the community alive once the meeting is over. They may need to appoint a co-ordinator and other roles, choose a communication mechanism, determine a meetings schedule, and begin a discussion on aims and objectives and ground rules. They will need to start up a membership list, and develop a plan for enrolling other members.

While extensive knowledge will be shared during the knowledge exchange you must plan to record that knowledge for the future and for those that can't be present. I will now look at recording knowledge at a knowledge exchange.

Recording

An enormous amount of knowledge will come out from a knowledge exchange. They are a very rich source of story, anecdote, experience, advice and guidance, and you need to capture this material in an equally rich way. Collecting bullet points from flip charts is not good enough! The whole exchange, including the smaller group sessions, will need to be recorded as close to verbatim as possible.

Use audio recording equipment

The best way to transfer knowledge is in the words of the people involved. When you come to package up the knowledge, then you need access to verbatim quotes and stories, and a transcript of the meeting will be the raw material you use. There is no real substitute for audio recording, though speed-writing or touch typing will also give a reasonably good result. I tried using shorthand secretaries at one point, but this did not work well as they were unfamiliar with the technical terms, and tended to leave these out!

If you are going to audio-record the meeting, you need to think carefully about the equipment you use. Placing cassette recorders in the middle of the tables, using the recorders inbuilt microphone, will not work. The recording will be dominated by motor noise, and people furthest away will be inaudible. Invest in table microphones, with adapters to feed them into the recorder, and place the microphones around the table so that all participants are close to a microphone. Make sure you have enough audio recorders to cover each group session (for example, if you intend to divide into six groups, you need six audio recorders and possibly 12 or 18 table mikes). Appoint people to operate the recorders.

Take detailed notes

Even if you record all the component parts of the knowledge exchange, you still need someone making fairly detailed notes, for the following reasons:

- You need to know who said what, so the quotes and recommendations can be attributed.
- Sometimes your recording equipment will fail, or the recording will be inaudible, and the notes are a backup.
- Sometimes it is culturally unacceptable to record meetings.
- Sometimes you will have divided the meeting into more groups than you anticipated, and will not have enough recording equipment for every group.
- The layout of the main room may make it impossible to record the feedback discussions.

If you have a number of small group discussions as part of the knowledge exchange, then you will need one note taker, or 'scribe', per group.

Take photographs

Knowledge transfer between people requires a degree of trust and relationship ('never accept knowledge from a stranger'). For this reason, it is important to do whatever you can to build links between the knowledge customer and knowledge supplier. Photographs build links. Take a digital camera and make sure you get a good picture of everyone present. Get hold of their contact details too; phone number, email, job title.

Video record the feedback sessions

Video is far more powerful than photographs in creating links between viewer and speaker, and are also a powerful means of capturing and sharing emotion. If a picture 'tells a thousand words', then video must tell millions. However, to video record an entire knowledge exchange would be a waste of tape and require a huge editing job. Video record the feedback sessions from the small dialogue groups, as these will be relatively short (10-minute) summaries of the discussions.

Identify and record 'people with a story to tell'

Identify, during the knowledge exchange, the people who have clear advice to give, and will give it simply and with emotion. Take them off to a quiet room during meal breaks or coffee breaks, and ask them to record a short 'piece to camera'. Record 1 or 2 minutes, 3 at the most.

Always ask for permission before recording a meeting

People can initially be very self-conscious about recording equipment, and it can make them guarded in what they say. Reassure them that the recordings are for transcription purposes only, and that they will have the right to veto anything before it is published. Once you have their permission to record, you will find they forget about the equipment within a few minutes.

Output

Consider the option of webcasting

There may be an advantage in webcasting the knowledge exchange; publishing it live (or semi-live) on to your corporate intranet, so that you can gather input from the rest of the organisation. If you have good internal communications, and the knowledge exchange covers a crucial topic that affects the entire organisation, then webcasting is well worth considering.

Build a knowledge asset

A knowledge exchange can be a good opportunity to collect all the knowledge needed to build a first-class state-of-the-art knowledge asset. The knowledge asset will contain rich content collected at the knowledge exchange, including multimedia, and will have the ownership of all the people at the exchange.

This is amply illustrated by the following extract from the General Motors case study contained in Chapter 12 that describes the challenge and their knowledge asset solution:

> Our second challenge was to devise a method for bundling and delivering groups of Best Practices to the appropriate Design Engineer. Since Authors deliberately wrote limited-scoped Best Practices (nuggets of knowledge), several Best Practices would be required to design a component or subsystem, Our solution is a Knowledge Set, an electronic 3-ring binder containing ...
>
> 1. *how-to* instructions,

2. a list of linked Best Practices (what, why, when, where and who),

3. linked short-cut access just the engineering product rule, and

4. a list of linked other technical sources like procedures, specifications, references.

Publish the knowledge asset

The knowledge that was shared at the knowledge exchange forms the raw material for a knowledge asset. Everyone who was present at the exchange will have a stake in this asset, and will be fascinated to see the end result. Try and publish as soon as you can (bearing in mind that it may take a month or two to process, edit and package everything).

Knowledge exchanges such as described above have been used by the BBC and General Motors. General Motors refer to them as Technical Exchanges and use them as part of the management of General Motors's Intellectual Capital management process. The BBC went a step further and created a physical centre for knowledge sharing, dubbed the SON&R. This was a dedicated facility provided for the BBC communities for hosting knowledge sharing events. Organising knowledge exchanges for 'hot topics' was part of the remit of the BBC knowledge management Champions.

Business driven action learning

Benchmarking may sometimes identify a performance area where the whole company is performing below the level it needs to. Instead of sharing knowledge within the company, new knowledge needs to be created or imported from elsewhere. In a case like this, a business driven action learning project should be considered.

Here a learning team is identified, who then engage on a programme of collective knowledge gathering, in order to learn how to improve company performance. The team usually glean learning from external sources. They can even learn from what their competitors are doing. For example, when a manufacturer of engineering valves decided to streamline their process and bring in lean manufacturing, they set up an action learning team to visit lean manufacturing sites in other industries, to gain knowledge of the principles, their application, and the issues around introducing lean, before starting their own internal programme. Also when BP Retail were introducing self-service retail stations in Japan, they set up an action learning programme to observe and learn from what their competitors were doing well, and doing not so well.

The keys to success in a business driven action learning programme are as follows:

- The team needs clarity about the topic and they need to research and to ensure it is a significant business challenge. The challenge can be broken down into subtopics, and individual team members can be given accountability for researching individual subtopics, but ultimately the emphasis has to be on collective learning.

- The team needs to seek knowledge from six areas:

  - Knowledge creators such as research centres, consultants and academics – Work with the best knowledge source. Be patient and ensure you have identified the RIGHT people to work with.

- Suppliers of technology and services. You need to build highly collaborative partnerships with suppliers and contractors, to fully exploit each others experience, knowledge and competencies.

- Regulators, both internal and external.

- Customers, to understand their needs, using the best user-group you can get to represent the internal and/or external customer population.

- The wider social environment, to learn what will be acceptable as a solution.

- Competitors, to gain as much knowledge as possible of the competitive environment.

- The team needs to consist of top quality operators who can interface with all the above groups. They need not have prior knowledge of the area that they are going to be learning about but must be open to new thinking and working in a collaborative fashion.

- The team needs to come together on a regular basis for team reflection and team learning especially when they have been removed from their normal work environment to conduct the business driven action learning. They will use learning visits and reflection sessions to capture knowledge, will apply AARs on a daily basis to keep their learning current, and will hold a retrospective at the end of the business driven action learning programme. They may package what they have learned into a knowledge asset.

- The team needs be trained in the principles of gathering knowledge. They need to be able to interview, to facilitate retrospects and AARs, and to express learning in terms of actionable advice for the future. Although the team undoubtedly have the right skills to deliver the project itself, they might not have the right skills for action learning, and they will need some training and co-ordination.

- The sources of knowledge, both internal and external, need to be briefed about the purpose of the action learning, and to help the learning team as much as they can. Obviously this won't happen if the team is trying to learn from competitors!

The process of business driven action learning consists of several cycles of learning from others, then bringing that learning together through AARs and retrospects. Ultimately this knowledge will be built into the team knowledge asset.

6

Communities of practice

Communities and informal networks exist in almost every organisation the reason being that humans have a need for social interaction. They naturally share tips on how to do things, shortcuts to make their job easier and generally make life easier for each other. Knowledge management harnesses this behaviour and makes it systematic. Communities can form the pipelines that allow knowledge and experience to flow from one part of the company to another and ensure that good practice in one plant has the opportunity to become best practice across the company. They are the vehicle that can allow peers to share and ask each other for help and assistance without being thought of as not being competent to do their job. Communities have the power to add considerable value in a services, operations and manufacturing environment. The model introduced in Chapter 2 shows the role that communities play as the interface between the activity of the operational or production units, and the corporate knowledge base.

Before I get into the detail on communities it might be worthwhile just pausing for a moment and identifying four assertions that apply to knowledge. These are:

- Knowledge is practice-related: knowledge is 'know-how'

– knowing how to practice, and how to perform operational tasks.

- Knowledge is dispersed: the practitioners around the company are the ones who know how to practice.

- Knowledge is communal: no one individual can know all there is to know about any area of practice.

- Knowledge is not static: as practice evolves, so does the knowledge.

The reason that I have suggested that these are assertions rather than facts is that I can't prove them to you on a scientific basis but I have found after many years in the field that they hold true in all organisations. These assertions imply that knowledge needs to be treated as community property, residing in a community, rather than being the property of experts. Knowledge is a community asset and needs to be treated as such.

In knowledge management terms, there are three distinct types of community, with different roles and account-abilities for knowledge management.

- Communities of purpose are funded teams, with accountability for the development of, or ownership of, a specific knowledge area.

- Communities of practice are networks of practitioners who share and apply knowledge with each other.

- Communities of interest are networks of individuals who receive knowledge and information from a central source.

Each type of community is summarised in Table 6.1, and discussed in more detail below.

Table 6.1	Comparison of communities

Community of purpose	Community of practice	Community of interest
Are committed to achieving a shared goal	Face common issues	Share a common interest
Members work together	Members work individually in their business units	Members may not work in the topic area
Members pool skills, time and effort	Members pool knowledge	Members pool information
Members deliver collectively	Members deliver separately	
Members assigned to the community by management	Free membership	Free membership
Community has a formal management structure	Informal management of the community by itself	Community isn't managed

The Orange case study (Chapter 12) shows this differentiation between community types, where a group of coaches have accountability for defining good practice (a community of purpose), and work with a selected subset of customer satisfaction staff and experienced customer reps (a community of practice) to discuss what that good practice might be. The rest of the customer reps and call centre staff are passive receivers of knowledge through the K-Village system, and form a community of interest. See Chapter 12 for details.

Communities of purpose

A community of purpose is one in which the members work together to deliver a common knowledge-related objective. They have many names – Aon Insurance calls them Global Practice Groups, BP calls them Delivery Networks, Rio Tinto calls them Centres of Expertise. Communities of purpose have a common purpose, and a common objective. They often have a budget, and collectively hold accountability for an area of corporate knowledge. They either develop the knowledge, through business driven action learning, or they maintain the knowledge through collecting and validating best practices and corporate standards. They own and maintain the corporate knowledge assets.

Communities of purpose generally comprise a small number of recognised subject matter experts. They operate as a team (often a virtual team, if the experts are from globally dispersed operational units), and use team-based knowledge management practices, as described in the companion volume 'Knowledge management for teams and projects'.

Communities of practice

A community of practice (CoP) was described by Stewart (1997) as 'a group of professionals within a corporation who are informally bound to one another through their exposure to a common class of problems and common pursuit of solutions. Members within the community of practice freely exchange knowledge which creates an even greater resource base of knowledge'.

The key points to note in this definition are that the community members share common issues and seek common solutions, and share knowledge with each other to improve performance in an informal way.

The value of a community of practice is to increase the effectiveness of its members. A CoP doesn't do this by creating a collective performance contract between its members and the business, but rather assists each member to deliver enhanced performance against his or her individual performance contract, by giving them access to the collective knowledge of the CoP, allowing them to solve problems more easily, and learn more quickly.

An example of this is shown in the story below. The use of electronic Q&A systems, as a means of making this easier, are further reviewed in Chapter 7.

Johnny's story

Years ago I was a shut-down engineer, and we were struggling with the topic of Systems Isolation and Control. Although we had been doing it locally for years, we had no idea how the rest of the company did it. I was going to give a talk on control of isolation points, and I realised that I only knew what we had done in our own local unit. So I quickly wrote an email to people around the organisation that I knew, simply asking 'Who knows about control of isolation points, what systems are out there? Because I have to give a talk next week. This is Thursday, I have to do it on Tuesday, so I have to prepare over the weekend'. Almost immediately I got two responses back from

---

within the same time-zone as myself in the UK.

Over the weekend I then received at least 6 different responses, and I was then able, over the Sunday night and across the Monday, to put together not only a Slide Pack, but also a briefing note detailing the best practice from across the company, We then went on to adopt that in our operating unit as a standard for isolation, which has then gone on to be shared out through the organisation. I was amazed actually at the speed of response. I had watched other people, but this was my own plea; it was me that needed help, and I was very pleased at the response from people that I didn't really know. I don't know how many times I thanked them for helping me, because it was a success

Membership of the CoP should be beneficial to the members. They should get more out of the CoP than they put into it. The value proposition goes hand in hand with the voluntary nature of CoP membership. CoPs that deliver value to the members will grow, as people voluntarily 'sign up'. Those that don't deliver value will shrink and die as the members 'vote with their feet' and leave. This is an excellent mechanism for weeding out the non-productive CoPs.

CoP's cut across organisational and geographical boundaries. Community members belong to both their business unit and to their community, and often feel a strong sense of 'belonging', giving them what might be called 'dual citizenship'. This sense of belonging provides trust within a community that assists knowledge to flow across, up and down the organisation.

The case studies described in Chapter 12 all discuss the role of communities of practice and how they are being used in each of the companies.

Community of interest

A community of interest is a community in which the members are more passive users of knowledge and information that is provided from a central source. Community members are users of knowledge, rather than creators, providers or sharers of knowledge.

Community tools and processes

When you launch your community, one of the things you will have to consider is how that community is going to exchange knowledge. Where the community is co-located, face to face meetings are the best vehicle to allow knowledge exchange. This was the model that DaimlerChrysler adopted with their Tech Clubs. The Tech Clubs were communities of practice dedicated to specific aspects of car design and manufacture, such as the Chassis Tech Club, the Braking Systems Tech Club, or the Sunroofs Tech Club. They met every week or second week, and spent an hour or two exchanging knowledge on common problems and seeking shared solutions.

If the community is not co-located then telephone conferences can be used to connect the members. Regular telephone conferences are a terrific method to keep the energy and 'connectedness' of the community members high. If the community members are dispersed across several time zones, care must be taken to share the pain of out of normal hours working across the members.

This might be combined with a Q&A system that allows members to ask each other for assistance. This topic is explored in more detail in the Technology section.

Technology is a support mechanism for the community rather than a community-building mechanism, and you should also plan for the members to meet face to face at least annually. While the main purpose of these gatherings is social and to allow members to reconnect with each other, they are frequently built around a knowledge sharing activity such as a knowledge exchange or a site knowledge visit.

7

The corporate knowledge base

The corporate knowledge base will have two components. First it will contain the established knowledge of the organisation. Secondly it will provide a holding place for new lessons.

An excellent example of the former is shown in the case study from General Motors (Chapter 12). Here, a knowledge base has been constructed over a number of years, containing over 4000 best practices, together representing the Technical Memory of the organisation. Each of these is owned by subject matter engineers, and constructed and validated by best practice teams.

In a similar way, the communities of practice ('Technical clubs') in Chrysler have constructed, and maintain, an 'Engineering Book of Knowledge' (EBOK) in 1997 as the corporate engineering knowledge base. The EBOK is web based with high security provisions such as encryption, password control, legal and other audits; print restrictions. It contains test data, quality data, standards, technical drawings and procedures. Access to the material in not permitted until after the material has been approved for use.

Another example of a corporate knowledge base from the car industry is the Ford Best Practice Replication (BPR system). BPR is a web-based system that collects good practices, approves them, and then assists them to be replicated and copied across plants as best practice. Since 1996, BPR has identified approximately $900 million in value and delivered over $590 million of that figure. It is reported that over 2700 proven practices have been collected and replicated more than 4200 times.

The BP Operations community maintains a library of corporate standards, guidelines and best practices, which supports the operations value process described in Chapter 12. This is provided via a corporate portal, which can be accessed by any corporate employee. Further details of the portal technology are provided in Chapter 8.

The BBC case study (in Chapter 12) describes knowledge assets; documented case studies and best practices stored on the BBC community intranet sites. Similar repositories of good practice are described in the CfBT Education Trust case study (see, for example, Figure 12.4).

Knowledge assets do not replace standards, procedures nor manuals but rather enhance them. The knowledge asset supplements and compliments these by providing access to the knowledge that the people who apply these standards and manual have gained.

The second component of the corporate knowledge base is provided by a Lessons Database. The technology behind these is described in further detail in Chapter 8.

Keys to a successful and effective corporate knowledge base are as follows:

- There needs to be clear ownership of the different areas of corporate knowledge. Subject matter experts need to be assigned, with clear ownership accountability (see Chapter 9).

- There needs to be a clear process for writing, organising and validating the knowledge. Usually the accountable owner will involve a community or practice, as described in the General Motors case study in Chapter 12.

- There needs to be a clear process for updating the knowledge base, by entering new lessons into the lessons database, and by updating best practices and standards in the light of new lessons.

- Rules have to be established on the use of local languages.

Another key factor in the introduction and sustainability of a successful corporate knowledge base is the ability of operations staff to be able to access it in real time. While for many organisations web-based access works very well this may not be the case in every instance. While you are at the design stage, give considerable thought as to how the corporate knowledge base is going to be accessed by the people that can get most benefit from it.

In some organisations there seems to be the assumption that the technology will self-organise and make available what people are seeking, via the appropriate search engine. Having been involved with on-line systems in several organisation where, quite literally, you couldn't find material that you knew was there, I would strongly council that you put in place a structure for the filing and retrieving of your material. Even the best search engine will not make up for bad filing behaviours.

One way of structuring the material is to think about the workflow or to associate the material with the activity being undertaken, e.g. store resources associate with 'production' under the heading of production. An alternative way it to file the resources associated with items of plant, e.g.

turbines, pumps, etc. Whichever way you decide, take your time over it and ensure that you have alignment with the people who will use the system.

I will now look at the BP Operations Excellence toolbox as an example of how an organisation can structure its knowledge.

The BP Operations Excellence toolkit is structured around the benchmark process described in Chapter 3. It is also structured around the level of validation that has been applied to the knowledge. At one level there is the highly vetted, approved knowledge in the form of corporate standards and required practices, which are referenced under the heading 'The BP Way'. At the opposite end of the spectrum is the knowledge in the Question and Response system, eCLIPS, which is totally unvetted. BP went a step further and provided a 'health guide' to the advice you were receiving.

Captured knowledge is presented in a hierarchy, as follows:

- **The 'BP Way'**: these tools describe the way BP does business (i.e. BP policy). This should be the first place to look when identifying ways (the 'what' and 'how').

- **Good practices**: these describe good practices identified for the relevant elements by either experience from operating assets (e.g. from OVP assessments, eCLIPS, etc.) or subject matter experts.

- **People**: these are people you can contact for help with closing your OVP score gaps for the relevant elements.

- **Communities**: these are communities of practice skilled in the relevant element.

- **eClips Community discussion forum**: this section links you to any questions (and responses) that have been asked about the relevant OVP element and allows you to ask the 'community' if you have been unable to find an answer in the toolkit. All entries in eCLIPS are purely voluntary and are not validated by subject matter experts. Community Q&A tools such as these are described below in Chapter 8.

This hierarchy is very important as it gives the reader a sense of how reliable the knowledge might be. Thus if the advice provided is in the form of The 'BP Way' then the reader knows that this is a fully validated and approved policy or procedure and can be followed with confidence. At the bottom end of the scale, advice provided via the eCLIPS system, which is not validated, needs to be treated with a lot more caution.

There are many ways of structuring knowledge within a knowledge base such as this one.

A popular structuring method is the FAQ, representing the most common questions that a knowledge-seeker will ask, plus reliable answers. An alternative structure is the toolbox containing details of tools and techniques that can be used. When structuring the knowledge, you should consider the end user of the resource and structure the content and layout to make it easier for the end user to be able to find what they want easily. For example, one organisation decided to structure its resource around the names of its customers, this however meant that you needed to know which customer had been supplied with what before you were able to access any of the corporate memory. Consider having multiple paths to find what the end user might be interested it.

8

Technology

In this section I will look at some of the technology that can assist you both to capture and share knowledge across the organisation. Technology should be seen as an enabler of knowledge management, not the focus of it

Portals, or knowledge libraries

These are technologies that support the first component of the organisational knowledge base, as described in Chapter 7. Most companies have a web-based system or portal. For example, Orange Call Centres use a website, K Village, to share learning with their training and learning specialists are responsible for its content. Access to lessons learnt and case studies of effective practice was also a key issue for the CfBT Education Trust. It was a key part of their communication plan for them to develop a corporate learning intranet site to store the lessons learnt. It was essential for them to be able to store not only the knowledge assets, but also to store core information and cross company business improvement projects within the same site.

Corporate intranets became more popular as

organisations started to realise that they could provide a simple route, via a web browser, to various company information and explicit knowledge. As the demand for the provision of portals increased, so to did the tools that the IT department could use to create and management content. Today it's not unusual for company employees to be able to publish direct to the company portal, and portals are becoming more and more customised to the needs of the individual user. Portals have also been seen as the way of integrating legacy applications in organisations, a situation that frequently occurs when one organisation is acquired by another.

As the understanding of the potential for portals to act as collaboration space across vendors and suppliers has increased, companies have now opened up parts of their portal to 'trusted' vendors and suppliers. This development allows the free flow of knowledge from those providing specialist services to the organisation and ensures that the corporate knowledge base is kept current.

An interesting and growing development in the field of portals is in part being driven by joint ventures and other such forms of collaborative working. In this situation two or more companies wish to be able to share and collaborate in a space without fear or contaminating the IT infrastructure of their parent company. To allow the free flow of information and knowledge in this partnership, portals hosted by third parties have been used. These hosted portals provide features such as databases, document management, email, shared diaries and discussion forums. From a knowledge management perspective, they allow the knowledge associated with that partnership to be managed for the benefit of the partners while keeping it intact from their respective parent companies.

Communities in Halliburton, the oilfield services

company, helped drive the development of portals in Halliburton. The communities wanted a space where they could collaborate to solve business problems and myHalliburton.com provided that. One of the key components was the Q&A area, details of which are given below.

Lessons learned databases

It may sound rather obvious but a lessons learned database (LLD) is a database that contains lessons learned. To be successful a LLD should have at least the following functionality:

- Easy input of lessons, within a taxonomy.

- A validation process.

- Keyword search. This should allow users to conduct broad searches using one or more key words.

- Menu search. This is a refined search and typically allows users to search within a specific area of the database as defined by the options given in the menu. For example, you might select bearings.

- Hybrid search. This is where a particular area of the database is to be searched using key words, e.g. bearings (menu) plus key words such as roller, high temperature.

It's preferable to structure your LLD around the topics, themes or work flow that the end users are accustomed to using. This allows users to easily identify where they should deposit a lesson, and makes it easier for others to retrieve them. If possible there should be one LLD per company or operation to ensure that the lessons learned in one functional area of the company are made accessible to all.

Many organisations will have two levels of LLD – a local one for the operational units in one factory or country, and a global one for the entire organisation (or for major functions within the organisation, such as operations, marketing or client service). The local LLD contains lessons applicable to that factory, or that country culture. The global LLD contains lessons of global applicability.

The intranet has meant that databases can now be searched irrespective of where the lesson has been learned. It is good practice to periodically review the content of the LLD to see if any patterns or themes are emerging. For example, you might find that a lot of lessons are appearing on the topic of working at height, and this might indicate that your training course needs to be updated in this area. The result of this review can also be used to update the best practices that are applied in the company.

Consideration should be given to creating standard templates for entering new lessons into the LLD. Templates make it easier to enter lessons to the database but also make it easier to search. A typical entry template is shown below, based on the four questions of the after action reviews (AARs will provide many of these lessons):

- *Title of the lesson.* This should make obvious to the reader what the lesson is about, a title such as 'lessons from failure of the high-load compressor' is better than 'lesson 245/ADE/47'.

- *Background context.* This is the context or background that the reader needs in order to be able to understand the situation that existed when the lesson was learned.

- *What happened.* Describe what happened and lead up to the lesson. Be as detailed as you can, use numbers, photographs and sketches to help the reader to understand what actually happened on the day you learned this lesson.

- *Root causes.* Here you discuss the reasons why the actual results occurred, and why they were different from expectation.

- *Recommendations.* This is where you move from historical description of what happened to outlining what you are suggesting should be done in the future. Be detailed and specific. These are your lessons.

- *Actions.* What are the actions arising from the lesson? The best lessons databases link through to an action tracking system, and also are able to link to the email system to forward the actions to the accountable people.

- *Contact details.* Insert your contact details so that someone who wants further details can contact you.

Note that the tone changes mid way through the template from recording what actually happened, to recommending to the reader what they should do in future to avoid this happening again. While understanding what happened is important, the key thing that the reader wants to know is what they should do differently to avoid this happening again (if it was something that went wrong) or what they should copy from you, in order to repeat the success you have outlined in the lesson. This is an important step and one that is frequently missed in lessons learned.

The language to be used in the LLD should also be considered. Initially, companies seem to have insisted that all entries to the LLD be in the official corporate language, to ensure that the entries were understandable around the organisation. There is a growing movement, however, to allow the use of local language and local LLDs. In this model, lessons are recorded in local LLDs in local language.

Periodically the LLD is reviewed and any lessons that are relevant to other plants are transferred to the corporate LLD in the corporate language. While this model is more complex, being able to record the lessons in their native language does encourage people to share what they are learning.

Yellow pages/people finders

Yellow pages/people finders are web-based directories that are used to identify and find people with particular skills and knowledge in an organisation. They differ from traditional telephone directories in that they are largely populated and maintained by the individual employees and that they provide an index of knowledge and expertise in addition to hard factual data such as email and telephone number.

I will now look at an example of a highly successful yellow pages system – the 'Sigma-Connect' system, marketed as Adept Solutions, and in place in many major organisations, including BP, Solvay and the BBC.

The system is personalised, in that it recognises you on log-in. As of February 2007, the BP system contained details of over 38 000 people. It allows you to search for individuals, for communities, and for knowledge topics. We will see how the knowledge topic search works.

Let us assume that I am looking for people with knowledge in the field of Drilling Engineering. Sigma-Connect allows us to choose this field of expertise from a pull-down list, and gives a list of subtopics, or more detailed areas of expertise. If I was looking for people with surveying expertise and knowledge in the field of Drilling Engineering I would select directional/surveying. This particular search actually finds 62 people in the organisation who say they have knowledge and experience in this particular topic. It is possible to e-mail any one of them, or to send a group e-mail to all 62. So for example, if you were facing a particular challenge to do with surveying an oil well, or if you had a particular question on surveying, then this is a quick way of finding 62 experienced people who may have useful help and advice for you.

Once you decide which of these people you would like to contact, you can click on their name and find their personal page. This contains some text describing themselves, their interests, employment history and a list of areas of knowledge and experience. The page also contains, near the bottom, their contact details and the names of members in their team. They may also have loaded a photograph of themselves.

Sigma-Connect also provides an index of the communities within the company. Each community has a community page, which describes the community terms of reference, the co-ordinator, the number of members, the most recent member, and its membership overlap with other communities, and so on. If you can, encourage people to personalise their photographs as it helps to create a sense of ownership and membership of the community.

A yellow pages system such as Sigma-Connect is an ideal way to allow operators to informally access the knowledge of the organisation by finding individuals to call or email, or to invite to a peer assist. If your company doesn't already have a yellow pages system, you should give serious thought to putting one in place.

eLearning

eLearning can be an effective way of transferring knowledge, in the form of online interactive teaching material. An eLearning system allows the user to progress at their own pace and to receive feedback on their progress and level of understanding.

There has been a proliferation of eLearning solutions on offer and the uptake by companies has been significant. The early eLearning solutions were electronic versions of classroom content and suffered from the lack of interaction that is the norm in the classroom. Typically there is a test at the end of each module and there was a tendency when the users 'failed' a test to recommend that they went back and redid the section that they had just failed on. More modern and sophisticated systems, however, recognise that this failure to pass the test at the end of the module could be down to several factors, including how the material was presented, the content itself and how the individual learns and assimilates material. These systems will then take the user down another route and present alternative material in a different way to help the user reach the desired level of understanding. The evolution in computer games has enabled eLearning to be presented in a very sophisticated format, which makes learning fun.

Where the knowledge of the operation or service can be codified, eLearning can be a useful component in transferring that knowledge, and eLearning sites can be linked into company portals and knowledge bases. More tactic knowledge will, however, be better transferred by processes such as peer assist, site knowledge visit and knowledge exchange.

Some examples of areas where eLearning has been successfully used include:

- To raise the profile of the BBC's editorial policy

- London Borough of Brent on how to provide good quality services to the public

- NHS Radiology where trainees can practise their diagnostic skills and compare their abilities to experienced practitioners

- Delivery of time-critical education to doctors on Pandemic Flu training.

Community question and answer forums

A Q&A forum has the ability to transform the way knowledge is shared within an organisation. Imagine you are facing an unfamiliar challenge in an operational situation and you suspect others have faced this challenge before. These are situations were Q&A forums come into their own, allowing you to ask a question of your peers around the company. Q&A forums are ideal support tools for communities of practice (see Chapter 6).

A Q&A forum will allow the user to post a question and ask the wider community of practice for assistance. A typical system will require the question to be posted via a website or portal, as this ensures that the question is filed and kept for future reference, and then the posting will be forwarded to the community members by email. Any community members who can help answer the question can click a link to post a reply. Generally, replies are collected on the website or portal.

Ground rules are important when establishing a Q&A forum. These might include:

- check that the question hasn't been asked before and only post your question if it's a 'new question'
- don't criticise spelling or use of language, not everyone is a native language speaker
- each question is valid, don't chastise for asking the question.

Halliburton, the oilfield services company has used Q&A forums to good effect. Previously they would have had specialist technicians flying around the world to assist local personnel with equipment problems. Today they use portals and Q&A forums to allow members of the community, irrespective of physical location, to ask for and share knowledge. One such community, consisting of 126 field technicians, reported that it had solved 684 technical issues in this way. Normally technicians help each other on topics such as equipment malfunctions and safety issues. Each community also has a knowledge broker, who is a specialist in that area of Halliburton's business, and who can also provide input to the responses supplied to questions from the field. The community also has a telephone backup for those who can't access the internet from their current location. This allows a question to be posted on their behalf and the response conveyed back to them.

The BP Q&A system for the operations community is called eCLIPS (discussed briefly in the previous chapter). eCLIPS was introduced to allow members of the operational community of practice (the Operations Excellence community) to access the knowledge of their peers worldwide.

eCLIPS works by email and arrives in the email inbox of the community members. BP had already learned that asking someone to go to a portal to answer questions didn't work. If the question and response system was to have significant uptake and usage it would have to send messages via the normal email inbox.

To use eCLIPS all you have to do is type your question into the appropriate box on the OE portal. Before the question is sent out, eCLIPS searches all previous questions and responses, databases, knowledge assets and other documents to see if the answer already exists. It provides you with a results screen as shown below.

At this stage other members of the community have not been involved in your request. If the information provided from the search doesn't provide the knowledge that you require, then you can send your question to the community.

When the community member responds to the email, the response is automatically sent to eCLIPS portal where it is filed and cross-referenced for future use, and an email response is sent direct to the person who raised the question. This avoids email inboxes being clogged by 'reply all' responses and ensures the response is saved for future users.

eCLIPS has another couple of neat features. All the people that reply to the question email are 'hooked' up together by the system so that they get notification of the other responses and in this way they are like a mini knowledge team, they are all interested in the subject. However, if you didn't know anything about the subject but were interested in the outcome, by saving the question in the facility call myCLIPS you are informed every time there is activity around the question.

With the eCLIPS system only 'new' questions are sent to the community via email, which radically reduced the email traffic. All the previous responses, plus all the documentation that the search engine can find, are stored for future users.

Asking the community for help

When you ask a question of the community you might not get back the response you expect. For example, someone once posted a question on the type of equipment to install to make nitrogen available to inflate car tyres. He was expecting responses such as 'install X as it's really reliable' or 'use T as it looks good', instead he was overwhelmed by responses that pleaded with him not to install the equipment at all. The community was concerned with nitrogen's reputation as the silent killer (you can't see, smell or taste it) and really challenged the individual as to the wisdom of installing such equipment.

Blogs

A blog is an online journal, published on the internet or intranet, where an individual (or potentially a team) keeps a public diary of text and graphics.

Blogs grew out of online diaries. The ability of anyone, anywhere to be able to share their thoughts on a daily basis seemed to touch a basis human need or desire and their use grew almost exponentially. Before too long people started to experiment with them in a business context. Blogs are a terrific mechanism to allow individuals to publish and broadcast their thoughts on a given topic to multiple readers.

The issue of validation is a key one, if blogs are to be used in knowledge management. Most blogs on the internet contain opinion, rather than valid knowledge. However, in an operational knowledge management setting, blogs could have the following uses.

- They could be used as online shift logs, for recording operator notes and observations to be transferred to the next shift.

- They could be used as a 'team learning diary' for a business driven action learning team.

- They could be used as a knowledge distribution mechanism for a community of practice leader.

Wikis

Essentially a wiki is a type of website that allows staff to edit, including adding and deleting, content. They are a collaborative tool that initially found favour among groups who were jointly creating complex documents, such as standards and manuals; however, as the technology has evolved, and the ease of use of wiki sites increased, they have started to be used to retain best practice in a form that allows it to be annotated by others.

For example, engineers in one manufacturing company are using a wiki to store and share knowledge about the operation and maintenance of conveyor belts. In another example, an oil company is using the knowledge of experienced operators to build a wiki on the subject of Bitumen production – a tricky process that requires considerable operator experience.

A good way of getting started with wikis is to put the current practice, or the current 'way of doing something', on to the site, and ask staff to contribute their experience and ideas on how to improve it. Through this process, it is possible to rapidly tap into a wide range of experience. Once the experiences have been shared and best practice developed, this should be taken off the wiki site and put somewhere more permanent.

One company, introduced wikis with the aim of allowing staff to share their thoughts and experience to create procedures or standards. They initially intended putting the current practices on the wiki as the starting point, but decided against it. The plan to introduce the wikis was well developed when the initial objections started to appear. Senior individuals were uncomfortable with the open access nature of wikis and they were very concerned that the opinion of a relatively junior person would have the same weight as that of a more experienced person. The project was shelved and wikis never became a working tool in that organisation.

Before you introduce wikis take time to think about the culture that is evident in your organisation. Wikis don't seem to do well in hierarchical, command and control type organisations or organisations that operate in a highly regulated environment. In other organisations they have proven to be a useful tool.

9

Roles

Clear roles and accountabilities are needed in any effective knowledge management system. These roles might include:

- corporate knowledge manager
- team knowledge manager
- knowledge management sponsor
- community facilitator
- knowledge management coach
- subject matter expert (SME).

Before I get started let me address a question that I am frequently asked, which is 'How do you select the right people for these crucial roles?'.

My advice is always to select someone for these roles based on two main criteria:

- a high degree of understanding and credibility within the business
- excellent communications and influencing skills.

Note that I haven't suggested selecting them based on the understanding of knowledge management. That's because I firmly believe that you can teach someone who meets the other criteria, the necessary knowledge management skills and techniques.

One client chose to select their knowledge manager based on knowledge management skills alone, and brought in an external knowledge management expert. It took that person over a year to get to grips with the way the organisation operated, and therefore to make an impact. You probably don't have the luxury of allowing a new knowledge manager a year to get to understand your business, so select them from within the company, based on the above criteria, and then teach them the knowledge management skills. This will be a far more effective approach than bringing in external consultants on long-term contracts to take the knowledge management roles.

The situation is slightly different when your organisation has been practising knowledge management for some time. In this situation you may find that you have a candidate who has excellent knowledge management skills but my advice would still be the same, if they don't meet the above two criteria, select someone else to be the knowledge manager.

Corporate knowledge manager

The role of the corporate knowledge manager is to set the strategy and direction of the company's knowledge management programme. They are the orchestra conductor, and working in conjunction with the business will identify the key knowledge that the company needs and the processes, technologies and accountabilities needed to manage that knowledge.

Business knowledge manager

The second level of knowledge manager is embedded within an individual business, production unit or site. They might be the new products unit knowledge manager, the knowledge manager for European marketing, or the Dakota Plant Knowledge Manager. Their remit will be much more specific, and focused on working with the business unit to achieve the targets established in the benchmarking process.

The BBC case study describes business knowledge managers (they called them 'Champions') who were volunteers from each of the four main regions. Their remit was to promote knowledge sharing in their respective regions and to support division wide activities selected by the nations and regions board as being strategically important. These included establishing strategic communities of practice, organising one-off 'hot topic' knowledge exchange events, and holding lessons learnt reviews.

Knowledge management sponsor

The knowledge management sponsor is the senior person, perhaps a board member, who will 'speak up' for knowledge management in senior meetings. They are the people who will ensure that knowledge management has adequate budget and resources and that it is seen as being a value-added activity for the organisation. The knowledge management sponsor need not be an expert in knowledge management but needs to have a commitment and passion for it. They also ensure that the knowledge management work is fully aligned with current and future initiatives. The knowledge management sponsor would normally be accountable for the application of the knowledge management framework.

Knowledge management coach

The knowledge management coach is a person who works with the front-line employees to help them to implement knowledge management in the workplace. They are the person who translates 'knowledge management processes and tools' into actions and activities that the operators can understand and implement.

The knowledge management coach is a people-centric personality who derives great reward from seeing others succeed. They tend to work in the background, educating, helping and assisting others achieve their goals.

It's important to be clear that the role of a coach is different from that of a trainer. Trainers are responsible for teaching, not coaching. Neither the coach nor the trainer should work in isolation from the other, but be seen as complementary and working together to achieve improvements.

The Orange case study (Chapter 12) describes the use of coaches in a Call Centre environment.

Community facilitator

In many ways the success of knowledge management in a continuous operations or production environment is dictated by the enthusiasm and skills of the community facilitators. One of the best community facilitators I have come across described himself as an 'energiser bunny' and by that he meant that his main role was to keep up the energy and participation level within the community.

A good community facilitator will be well known and respected by the community that they facilitate and should, ideally be a member of that community. Some of the responsibilities of the co-ordinator include:

- managing the community discussion (online, and face to face)
- making sure agreed community behaviours are followed
- setting up community meetings
- working with the core group within the community
- liaising with the company subject matter experts
- watching for problems where knowledge sharing is not happening
- maintaining the membership list
- representing the community to management
- managing the life cycle of the community
- keeping energy levels high among participants, to ensure active participation
- working with the subject matter experts to ensure the community knowledge base is properly maintained and managed.

Subject matter experts

Subject matter experts (SMEs) are the owners of a specific knowledge area. They are accountable for ensuring that the knowledge associated with their area of expertise is kept current, and made available to those who need it. The SME needs to be an active member of the community to ensure that they are aware of the developments in the application of the company's knowledge.

There can be a temptation of appoint the SME as the community facilitator but this should be avoided in normal circumstances. It is preferable to have the SME actively involved and contributing to the knowledge of the community rather than spending their time organising and maintaining the community.

The General Motors Case study (Chapter 12) contains useful insights to the role of the SMEs. They use the term SMRE (subject matter responsible engineer) for this role. In addition they have other roles related to the development of the knowledge base, such as the best practice author and approver as well as the knowledge asset manager (KAM). See the General Motors case study for further details.

Librarians and cybrarians

These roles are responsible for maintaining the framework, taxonomy and structure of the corporate knowledge base. They don't own the content – this is owned by the SMEs – but they make sure the content structure is maintained, allowing it to be easily accessed.

Roles in a legal services context

(Text provided by Jessica Magnusson, Baker & McKenzie.)

Professional Services firms such as legal firms may appoint knowledge management roles as outlined below. These include Professional Support Lawyers (PSLs), Professional Support Paralegals, and Know How Partners.

Professional Support Lawyers

The PSL role has developed in the UK over the last 20 years and is today a well established role within law firms in the UK. In other countries the PSL concept is, however, new or relatively unknown. International firms, such as Baker & McKenzie, are recognising the value of PSLs and are expanding their PSL network at a global level. PSLs are usually non-fee earning, senior lawyers who ensure that their client-facing lawyers have the tools they need to serve their clients. They support the fee earning lawyers in different ways, depending on the practice areas' requirements. Their work tends to fall into three broad categories – know how (e.g. advice and consultation to lawyers, precedents drafting, legal updates and newsletters, intra- and extranet maintenance); training (e.g. internal and external training on legal development); and business development (e.g. pitch support, client alerts, client seminars). Some do a mix of all areas, others specialise in one or two of them.

Many law firms have their PSLs embedded in legal departments, with a few PSLs working in the central knowledge management department or Library. In the London office of Baker & McKenzie, they use a hybrid model. All PSLs work in the legal departments, and are close to departmental business objectives, yet can pull upon the support of appropriately skilled professionals within the central knowledge management department when required.

Professional Support Paralegals

The Professional Support Paralegal supports the PSLs by, for example, dealing with specific research enquiries that require legal expertise and interpretation, capturing and disseminating know how, and assisting the PSLs and fee earners in general.

Know How Partners

At Baker & McKenzie, London, the Know How Partners are fee earning partners with an additional responsibility for overseeing the knowledge management objectives and plans within their legal departments.

Librarians

One of the aims of the knowledge management department of Baker & McKenzie, London, is to ensure that the PSLs have as much time as possible to focus on those areas other support personnel cannot perform, e.g. precedent drafting, technical legal training and the provision of guidance notes. To assist in this, Professional Support Librarians provide support to the PSLs ranging from the provision of business information and monitoring legislative changes to knowledge management system cataloguing and maintenance. Firms that have this role report that it creates more time for the PSLs to concentrate on their core know-how responsibilities, but it is also the most efficient means of completing this kind of work.

The roles of operations technicians in knowledge management

Much of the above text has been about defining accountability for making learning happen. At the end of the day, however, someone has to go and do the learning.

My preference is always to involve the people who will use the knowledge in the learning process itself. If you are going to maximise the potential of the workers you need to engage them in the acquisition of the knowledge they will need. Align what is created with the processes they already have. The front-line technician can be a very powerful force in your drive to improving your performance. If you don't engage the people at your front line then no matter what you try to do, it will almost certainly fail.

Operations technicians already share knowledge; if a piece of bad news about wages comes from head office, most of your technician teams will know all about it by the end of the day, even the teams off shift! So it is about tapping the process that already exists and using it to open up the dialogue that will let the sharing happen.

I have encountered many examples of how technicians have been involved in the knowledge sharing process but the most prolific area seems to be that of Health, Safety and Environment. There are no competitive advantages to be had in hoarding your safety knowledge, and individuals and companies will freely share what they know. Perhaps this is the area that you should first engage with your operations staff. Learn how to share and re-use knowledge in this arena before moving on to potentially more commercially sensitive areas.

Sometimes it is the simple things that can make a big difference to the operations staff and this is one of these: at one site gas detectors were routinely used but the area where they were recharged was generally untidy, with cables and chargers located randomly. One technician decided to build a board and systematically mount the chargers by type and generally produce a more user-friendly system. Not only is the new board more tidy but it instantly lets the control room staff see how many of the portable gas detectors are out on site and encourages the user to return the detector to the appropriate charger. The design and material of this board have now been circulated to other control rooms as an example of good practice.

Assurance and monitoring

See Figure 2.1 for the model for knowledge management in operations, production, manufacturing and services. If this cycle of learning and performance is to be maintained, the company must have some way of monitoring and assuring that this cycle is being applied effectively to improve performance.

This assurance may have the following components:

- knowledge management standards
- knowledge management plans
- knowledge management monitoring.

Knowledge management standards

In order to successfully embed knowledge management in your organisation you will have to establish a minimum standard or expectation for knowledge management, that everyone will work to. Currently there are no international standards for knowledge management, so you will need to develop standards of your own.

You need to take a very pragmatic approach. If your requirements are overdemanding there is a very real danger that the business will reject them and refuse to comply with them. You should aim to create a minimum set of requirements that provides sufficient structure but isn't a burden on the organisation. For a continuous environment the knowledge management minimum standard might include:

- a performance learning review at the end of each year (or other planning cycle)
- annual performance benchmarking
- establishment of a goal or target for at least one key performance area
- a knowledge management plan that outlines how you are going to close the gap.

Knowledge management plans

These are documents that define the key knowledge that an operational unit will need to deliver its performance targets, where that knowledge will be sourced from, who will be accountable for acquiring that knowledge, and how any new knowledge will be captured and shared with other units.

The knowledge management plan makes tangible not only the knowledge, but also the process by which that knowledge will be managed. In many ways it is similar both in concept and format to risk management plans, but rather than identifying and articulating how the business-critical risks will be managed, I am now applying the same rigor and discipline to defining how the business-critical knowledge will be managed.

The categories chosen for performance measuring and benchmarking will define the key tactical knowledge areas for each unit's knowledge management plan. The benchmarking data will also identify the sources of that knowledge (i.e. the high performing units). The knowledge management plan also needs to define the actions that will be taken to acquire the knowledge (such as a knowledge site visit, a peer assist or a knowledge exchange), and will also assign the accountabilities for these actions. In this environment it is important to remember that the accountability should ideally be placed with the person who will be applying that knowledge. For example, if the knowledge is about maintenance, then the accountability for acquiring maintenance knowledge should be delegated to the senior maintenance person. If it's about power use, then it should be delegated to the senior electrical engineer.

The knowledge management plan should be regularly reviewed as part of the management assurance process.

Knowledge management monitoring

This is a process where by the current state of knowledge management in the organisation is 'measured'. There are three types of monitoring: (1) at the level of the local operational unit; (2) at the level of the community of practice; and (3) at the level of the organisation.

1. *Monitoring the local operational unit.* Monitor the local operators' familiarity with knowledge management tools and processes, and monitor how those tools and processes are being applied. Review the use of the knowledge management plan, and how this is being applied and updated. The focus will be very much at the local operational level and will almost entirely ignore the corporate or cross business situation.

2. *Monitoring the community of practice.* This will focus on

assessing the growth and activity levels of the community. It will look at the type of questions that are being asked and answered by the community members within the Q&A forum. The frequency at which the stored knowledge of the community is updated, and the quality of that knowledge, will also be monitored.

3. *Monitoring knowledge management within the organisation.* This will focus on assessing the levers and barriers that aid or impede knowledge management and on monitoring the achievement of the organisation's knowledge management or learning goals. It will also monitor the use of the benchmarking process and the effectiveness of the technologies provided. The balanced scorecard described by CfBT Education Trust (Chapter 12) is a means of monitoring the level of organisational knowledge management.

The use of an audit-based monitoring process allowed General Motors to identify that lessons in the North American lessons learned process were not being consistently addressed. This resulted in the lessons learned process being replaced with a more visible learning process, which they entitled, 'Closed-Loop Learning'. Further details are contained in the case study in Chapter 12.

Knowledge management metrics

Metrics should be part of the monitoring process. For example, General Motors report the number of best practices viewed by region as well as the percentage of best practices viewed by author/reviewer and design engineer. Monitoring usage such as this allows them to aim to revise about one-third of the best practices each year.

The linkage with other management disciplines

Six sigma

Six sigma has its origins in defect management and quality management. The term came to prominence in 1989 when Motorola announced a step change in its defect rate. The claim changed the way quality was perceived and quickly led to others following Motorola's lead. To understand six sigma and its aspiration, it's important to briefly touch on its origins.

In any manufacturing process there will be defects. The closer you are to producing all your products to specification, the higher your sigma number will be and the higher your yield will be for a given amount of input material. In layman's terms, at three sigma there will be 66 810 defects per million, at four sigma there will be 6210 defects per million and at six sigma there will be 3.4 defects per million. The desire to operate at six sigma is clearly illustrated by these numbers but so to is the challenge to operate at that level.

Six sigma moved from a measure of quality and control of defects into a mantra that indicated the desire of a company to be best in class at whatever it undertook. At its core was a quantifiable or measurement-based strategy that established the current situation, the desired outcome and a plan to move to close the gap. It is a very structured approach and makes considerable use of the experience of operators to contribute to the plan that closes the gap.

A typical six sigma project will follow a six-step process:

- define the problem
- measure the current situation
- analysis
- plan to improve
- pilot/monitor changes
- transfer to other plants/areas.

I would now like you to view the above six steps but this time add in the knowledge management concepts and processes discussed above. The results might look something like:

- define the problem (and identify what knowledge needs you have)
- measure the current situation (and establish the benchmark)
- analysis (where will the knowledge come from)
- plan to improve (create the knowledge management plan and set targets)
- pilot/monitor changes (learn from others using the knowledge management processes, share learning with community)
- transfer to other plants/areas (publication of lessons).

To me this shows quite clearly that six sigma and knowledge management can be very closely aligned. What knowledge management does, is define the learning dimension within six sigma. Whenever you are doing a six sigma activity you should be making maximum use of the knowledge within the organisation. The roles that are used in six Sigma can also be equated to roles in knowledge management. For example, a master black belt could equate to a subject matter expert, if they were expert in the topic area as well as the process, or it could equate to a knowledge manager if they are only managing the process itself. The various 'belts', e.g. black and green, form the community of practice around six sigma.

I believe that the success of six sigma is based on two key things: the inclusion of operators in understanding the current situation and designing the desired outcome, and a quantitative approach. It is no coincidence therefore that the knowledge management model for continuous operations offered in this book includes these two components.

Lean operations

There are several definitions of lean operations or lean manufacturing but I tend to favour the very simple one; lean is the elimination of waste and things that don't add value, as defined by the end customer. For me, the last part about the end customer is vital. You may have the best and most efficient manufacturing plant but if you aren't delivering the right product to the customer on time, then so what? Lean operations will therefore operate with less; less inventory, less defects, less time to develop a new product.

Value stream mapping is a key element of lean operations and creates an overview of the entire process by mapping the individual activities and processes that make up the overall process. In doing so waste is identified and hence opportunities to eradicate that waste are highlighted. Numerical methods, similar to those used in six sigma, can be used to highlight waste areas. For example, data such as – time (cycle time, delay time, queue time, set-up and changeover time); errors (data entry); distances travelled (by people, parts, materials, tools); queues (number, length, duration) – can all be used to understand where the waste is occurring in the overall process. In many operational situations, the time to set-up and changeover can also hide waste.

While numerical processes can and are used to help to understand where the waste might lie, the lean operation philosophy is not totally dependent on numerical analysis. BP's Operations Excellence Group created a mythical character, The Phantom, as the focal point of its waste elimination programme and used strap lines such as, 'How do we eliminate the Phantom', to reinforce the numerical approach.

Lean operations have plenty of scope for the inclusion of knowledge management tools and techniques. Lean encourages the use of communities, benchmarking and the sharing of knowledge and experience. All it takes to include knowledge management in a lean operations programme is to start to think about things through a knowledge lens and ask yourself questions such as, 'What knowledge do we have that could be applied to this?' and 'Who should we share our new learnings with'?

Companies such as Ford have expanded beyond their own factory walls to share best practices with partners and suppliers and hence eliminate waste throughout the value chain. Ford's total cost management (TCM) centre conducts reviews and workshops to help optimise consumer value on its vehicles. The centre is co-located with key management of the cross-functional plant vehicle teams with the view to improving communications and facilitating problem solving with the plant-based teams.

Quality management, total quality management and quality circles

Total quality management (TQM) is a management approach based around quality. TQM is a philosophy, a way of thinking about goals and processes, but is not a system, a tool or even a process. TQM applies to all departments and aspects of the organisation and not just to those who produce a product. Tools that are used in TQM include flowcharting, statistical process control, Pareto analysis, cause and effect diagrams and satisfaction surveys. Techniques that are used include:

- benchmarking
- cost of quality
- failure mode effects analysis
- piloting.

Once the current status has been measured and agreed upon, targets are set and worked towards. TQM must be seen as being as an integral part of the day to day activity of any organisation and not an 'add on'.

ISO 9000 is a Quality System Management Standard. TQM is a philosophy of perpetual improvement. The ISO Quality Standard sets in place a system to deploy policy and verifiable objectives. An ISO implementation is a basis for a total quality management implementation. Where there is an ISO system, about 75% of the steps are in place for TQM. The requirements for TQM can be considered 'ISO plus'. Another aspect relating to the ISO Standard is that the proposed changes for the next revision will contain customer satisfaction and measurement requirements. In short, implementing TQM is being proactive concerning quality, rather than reactive.

Of the 10 steps that are normally followed in TQM, the ones that are of most interest to us from a knowledge management perspective are:

- pursue a continuous improvement strategy
- use a structured approach.

Again the links with knowledge management are strong in that a typical TQM programme would describe the following steps to process improvement:

- measure the current situation
- analyse
- identify areas for change
- pilot changes and monitor impact
- communicate changed process.

TQM also encourages front-line workers to be intimately involved in defining the problem and the potential solution. Indeed this 'empowerment' of the workforce is a key component of TQM. Provided that the workforce use learning in identification of improvements, then knowledge management and TQM can be linked.

Another process that is frequently used in TQM and other quality initiatives is the quality circle. A quality circle is usually made up of volunteers who meet to discuss improvements to their work activities. The outcome of these discussions is presented to management for their approval and permission to move into action. Quality circles have been used on topics such as safety, manufacturing processes and product design and have the advantage of continuity in that the circle is not dependent on the activity or project being worked on at present. Quality circles tap into the knowledge of the workforce and provide a mechanism to focus their potential creativity into new solutions. In some ways a quality circle is like a mini-community of practice in that everyone is giving some of their knowledge but improving their overall knowledge in return. Quality circles can also make use of other knowledge management processes such as benchmarking, peer assist, knowledge exchanges and site knowledge visits. It is easy to see how one quality circle might visit another site to see how they undertake an activity and bring that knowledge back to their own site. Quality circles can also use knowledge management techniques such as business driven action learning.

Risk management

The management of risk is a well-known activity and discipline in many organisations. It is not unusual to find that the company or division has a risk register that not only defines the risks currently perceived to be facing the organisation, but also gives details of how those risks will be proactively managed by the organisation. The risk register is normally updated quarterly and included in the management reporting system of the organisation.

Risk management and knowledge management can be closely linked. The acquisition of knowledge is often the most effective way of reducing risk. It is important to remember that the risk may be internally or externally driven and the knowledge that you will need and where that knowledge may come from could be significantly different in each case.

The process that an organisation follows to manage risk might look like:

- clarity on the strategic goals of the organisation
- risk assessment (identification, potential size or consequence of the risk)
- analysis (probability, potential impact, ranking)
- ranked risk register (ranking and management of the risk)
- monitoring and refreshing
- review and reporting.

An excellent way of managing risk is to identify the knowledge that you need to manage that risk. Let's consider an example. Suppose one of the risks facing your company is 'product contamination'. Now view this through a knowledge lens and ask yourself 'What is the knowledge that I need to be able to proactively manage that risk?' You should be able to identify that knowledge and also where that knowledge is going to come from. In our example the knowledge that you need might include how to:

- handle the material to prevent contamination
- store the material to prevent contamination
- ship the material to prevent contamination
- define the training requirements for the operations staff
- train operations staff
- ensure competency of the staff
- ensure compliance with the procedures.

Managing your knowledge is an excellent method to manage risk.

Health, safety and environmental management

The approach that is taken to health, safety and environmental (HSE) management can be either to be very prescriptive and define what must be done and when, or alternatively may define expectations that must be met, and leave the division or the individual the flexibility to determine exactly how they are going to deliver that expectation. In either approach you will need a lessons learned system.

While having a lessons learned system is a fundamental aspect of managing safety it is by default a reactive system, e.g. something has to have gone wrong or an incident has to have occurred, before it becomes a lesson. The key is learning from that incident or lesson and proactively managing safety to avoid those incidents from occurring in future.

Risk assessment and risk management are the proactive side of HSE management. They are focused on the identification of hazards, the assessment of the risk and actions that can be put in place to manage those risks and prevent them becoming a near miss or accident. A key component of this are the data that are collected from near misses and accidents and their investigation. Understanding the root cause behind the data can allow proactive management to be put in place. For example, as a result of a number of near misses, one organisation realised that its training on entry into confided spaces wasn't as good as it could be. A review of internal and external practice resulted in a new procedure being developed and then rolled out across the entire organisation together with appropriate 'hands on' training.

Measurement is an important part of any HSE system as it enables progress to be charted. Most companies have an HSE audit/monitoring process that will report on the current situation and this can form the basis of a knowledge management system if these metrics can be used for benchmarking. Fluor Inc. uses its network of HSE professionals and site managers to update its incident reporting system to provide senior management with real-time information on HSE performance. A monthly summary highlights compliance with HSE systems and reports on each business unit performance. Summaries such as these are used to proactively target knowledge that either needs to be acquired or further disseminated to be more effectively utilised within the businesses.

A good HSE management system can therefore be closely linked with a knowledge management system. Knowledge management processes such as peer assist can be used to obtain learning that can be shared with others. HSE management also has the advantage in that companies do not perceive it as giving them competitive advantage and will freely share their learning with other companies. HSE management is a great area to demonstrate to senior management the value of learning from others.

Performance management

This is strategic in nature and needs to address the broader issues facing the organisation. It has long-term goals and includes performance improvement through the continuous development of individuals and teams. It also focuses on encouraging behaviours that will foster better working relationships. Performance management also has a harder edge to it in that it is also about planning and measuring. 'If you can't measure it, you can't manage it and if you can't manage it, you can't improve it' could well be the subtitle to the heading of performance management. Above all else, performance management is a continuous process and not a special one-off event.

Performance management should affect all employees and as such needs a framework to be effective. Corporate strategic goals provide the starting point for business and departmental goals, followed by agreement on performance and development, leading to the drawing up of plans between individuals and managers, with continuous monitoring and feedback supported by formal reviews. Performance management also makes extensive use of goals and targets frequently linking them into a date by which they have to be achieved. In knowledge management terms this would be the benchmarking and target setting stage of our model.

As with any measurement system care must be taken when determining what to measure in a performance management system. Be careful that you don't fall into the trap of measuring what's easiest to measure or measuring too many things, as discussed in Chapter 3. The measurement should also reflect the job/seniority of the person being measured. Simple output measures might be adequate for a production worker but not for a senior manager.

Interestingly, performance management is frequently linked with pay via performance-related pay schemes. If this is the case, ensure that you reward collaboration and overall performance improvement rather than one individual or team's improvement. At the end of the day you want the overall performance of your organisation to improve by the sharing and re-use of knowledge with people being rewarded for that.

The General Motors case study reports that writing and sharing best practices is an integral part of the subject matter expert's job and is reflected in their performance reviews, part of the General Motors performance management process and is linked to salary merit increases and bonuses.

Case histories

The model described above illustrates what I believe to be the ideal approach to KM in service, operations and production. The following case studies show various examples of how different companies have addressed this issue.

BBC Production and Services

The Nations & Regions Sport Community of Practice, by Claire Garwood, previously of the BBC 'Live and Learn' team, now a Knowledge Executive with a major company.

Context

The BBC's central KM team was established during 2000 with two purposes; firstly to introduce social tools to foster knowledge sharing, and secondly to provide advice and support to managers and leaders wishing to promote knowledge sharing. In 2001 the Nations & Regions ('N&R') Board approached the KM team for help with a divisional knowledge sharing plan. N&R is the largest division in the BBC and at the time employed nearly 7000 staff (around 27% of the BBC's workforce). N&R faced challenges with knowledge sharing as its 50 sites are spread across the United Kingdom, with 40 English local radio stations, 6 dedicated radio stations for Scotland, Wales and Northern Ireland and several regional television centres. The geographical situation is compounded by the demands of a continuous operation, with staff frequently out on location. However the common challenges faced by staff doing similar work presented a fertile, receptive ground for encouraging more systematic knowledge sharing. N&R staff had begun to organise frequent local knowledge sharing events and the N&R Board felt some strategic steer would maximize their success.

The champion model

A champion model was agreed whereby four Good Practice Leaders ('GPLs') were recruited internally on a voluntary basis from Scotland, Wales, Northern Ireland and England. Their remit was to promote knowledge sharing in their respective regions and to support division-wide activities selected by the N&R Board as strategically important. This included establishing strategic Communities of Practice ('CoPs'), organising one off 'hot topic' knowledge exchange events and lessons learnt reviews.

The GPLs received a budget and 20% of their time (one day per week) to spend exclusively on their GPL role. An N&R Board member line managed their activities and the KM team (six staff) provided one consultant for 75% of their time. We subsequently called our model the 'windmill model' (see Figure 12.1 below) which accidentally emerged as I drew a picture of how N&R knowledge sharing initiatives were linked via the GPLs..

Figure 12.1   The BBC 'Windmill' diagram

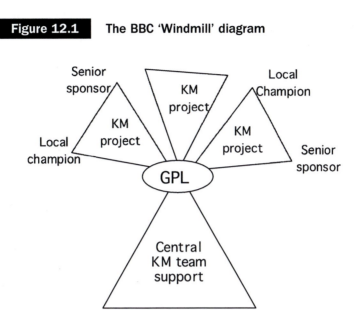

The GPLs were the central pivot for knowledge sharing in N&R for a variety of reasons:

- dedicated budget
- protected KM time
- personal performance objectives
- strategic support from the N&R Board
- back-up from the KM team.

We also insisted each initiative had a senior sponsor to ensure credibility, and a local champion who was delegated authority by the senior sponsor to deliver the initiative. (The latter idea was in fact provided by a non-BBC contributor at an unrelated knowledge exchange.) This structure sometimes made it complicated to explain how everything links together – hence the diagram. With knowledge sharing you can sometimes have a lot of hot air and no action. This model not only shows the relationship between the parties involved but it also reinforces the message that dedicated support is required to harness this energy and turn it into something that works well.

KM Training

To get the GPLs started the KM team ran a 2 day workshop on knowledge sharing fundamentals. This included:

- Defining knowledge sharing and its role in the BBC
- Building a case for knowledge sharing – what are the benefits?
- Basic knowledge sharing techniques (after action reviews, knowledge exchange sessions etc.)
- Identifying priority areas for knowledge-sharing

The GPLs' initial tasks were largely ambassadorial, so the training aimed to enable them to talk with authority and enthusiasm about the benefits of knowledge sharing. The KM team would then provide tailored support as specific initiatives began. This eventually included:

- Identifying and scoping knowledge needs for particular groups or activities
- Selecting appropriate knowledge sharing solutions (e.g. communities, blogs, wikis)
- Designing and facilitating face to face knowledge sharing activities
- Packaging and publishing knowledge assets for re-use

The Sport community launch

N&R staff producing sport output across television, radio and online were one of the first areas to benefit. Knowledge sharing was ad hoc and of limited impact, so the KM team advised that a strategic CoP would ensure systematic, focused knowledge sharing.

Four 'Sport Good Practice Champions' were nominated by the N&R Heads of Sport as community hosts to represent England, Scotland, Wales and Northern Ireland. Like the GPLs, their remit was to foster both local and divisional knowledge sharing. The sport champions canvassed local opinion to identify hot topics for knowledge sharing. They then liaised with the GPLs and KM team who designed and subsequently facilitated a one and a half day community launch event in Autumn 2002. Around thirty N&R sports staff were nominated by their line managers to attend. Their departments paid their travel and accommodation costs but all other event costs were funded centrally. This ensured people made the most of the time away from their day jobs as they had a stake in the funding.

The event began with each region show reeling content they felt exemplified innovative output or excellent use of existing good practice. BBC staff are naturally curious (and competitive!) of one another's output and always proud to discuss their own. This activity was therefore well within their comfort zone. Throughout the day a mixture of plenary and break out groups enabled knowledge sharing on hot topics. The KM team also specifically planned numerous, ample breaks to enable informal networking – again something that BBC staff are particularly adept at because it is a critical programme-making skill.

A key win was the enthusiasm of the Director of N&R to attend dinner and speak about the importance of knowledge-sharing. Dinner also involved teams competing for a prize by re-enacting coverage of any sporting event in history using knowledge acquired during the event. Hilarity ensued and it was a fun way to cement relationships and reinforce people's learning. The final morning involved action planning ideas generated at the event.

The Sport community early years

The community launch was a great success and is now an annual calendar event. Different staff are nominated to attend each time to cross fertilise relationships. After the first event, each champion also began organising sub-group activities. These aimed to meet specific needs in either their home areas or cross-divisionally. For example, sports commentators have held their own events.

The BBC had centrally funded a variety of social networking tools including blogs, wikis, online discussion areas and a staff yellow pages. Interestingly the sport community chose instead to communicate via shared email distribution lists in between face to face events. This was frustrating as it meant any knowledge shared was confined to their community when it may have been of use to other groups in the BBC.

This was not unusual for the BBC; culturally email is the preferred mode of communication when in-person meetings aren't possible and people usually rely on networking with individual or group contacts. This was the trade-off for the group developing a strong identity. However within the community it ensured the impetus remained. Group emails enabled members to hear about things happening outside of formal community events, even if it wasn't in their own area. Later, a community intranet was established which centred around a location advice database on sporting venues. This was populated by community members.

The Sport community matures

The Sport champions quickly gained confidence and only sought help from the GPLs (and by extension the KM team) on the design and facilitation of their annual community event. This risked their lessons learnt not being passed back to the GPLs and KM team. Fortunately the KM team had in place two mechanisms to mitigate this risk.

Firstly, as part of the KM team's wider work across the BBC, they ran a website which published knowledge assets captured from activities they supported. Each activity was also profiled so people had access to 'KM about KM'. A monthly e-bulletin was then set up which staff could subscribe to receive. Over time the list grew to several thousand and was a popular resource. Subscribers included people interested in knowledge sharing, people who wanted to use the published knowledge or who simply wanted to keep up to date with what was going on in other areas of the BBC.

The KM team therefore ensured they made regular contact with the Sport champions to issue press releases on Sport community activities. This maintained lines of communication at times when no KM support was required and also show-cased their good work to the rest of the BBC.

Secondly, though much later, the KM team introduced a formal KM curriculum which included a workshop entitled 'Hosting a Community'. Some Sport champions attended the workshop, despite the fact they initially declined to receive any coaching or tips on hosting. With hindsight perhaps this was obvious. Natural networkers find it easy to kick off events. However its sustaining interest across a large group that's the challenge.

N&R knowledge-sharing matures

The value of knowledge-sharing in N&R was proved very quickly. The N&R Board eventually invested in the creation of a physical centre for knowledge-sharing at its Bristol site, dubbed 'SON&R' (Sharing Opportunities Across Nations & Regions). At the centre all communities, including Sport, now have dedicated facilities to host knowledge-sharing events. This is complemented by an Executive Group who meet several times each year to ensure SON&R's activities meet strategic priorities. A User Group of N&R representatives also discuss and provide the Executive Group with ideas for activities. Due to SON&R's success, the 4 GPL roles were subsumed into its activities in 2004. Local champions continue however to lead certain communities across N&R.

What we learnt

Don't be pushy; use Schein's process consultation principles

This means being opportunistic and ensuring that every interaction is helpful. In N&R this involved not being proud about the type of support provided; typing flip chart pads of knowledge exchange events for busy community hosts was just as important as facilitation and event design. Loaning out KM team members is also a great way to build relationships and foster knowledge flow.

Use organisational culture to its advantage

Select approaches that enable people to stay within (or to step just outside of) their cultural comfort zone. BBC staff are naturally excellent networkers. This meant they would foster excellent CoPs provided they had the focus and support from dedicated community hosts.

Use local language, not 'KM speak'

This case study is written using KM terminology as it has an informed readership. In contrast the BBC's N&R Sport champions simply saw themselves as people who wanted to improve their story telling by meeting more regularly to discuss their output. The KM team did not therefore talk about 'strategic CoPs with hosts promoting knowledge sharing' as this would have not have meant anything to them at a personal, local level.

Capture and publish learning about knowledge sharing as it happens

This is particularly important – but difficult – when your help is no longer required with ongoing activities as those involved become self sufficient. You can't foist yourself onto people so an easier inroad to maintaining contact is to ask if you can learn from the great work they are doing. People always appreciate recognition of their efforts. Further, profiling their activities via e-bulletins draws in people who aren't yet interested in knowledge sharing but want to keep up to date with what's going on.

Don't be afraid of focusing efforts on CoPs that are already taking off

The most successful CoPs are usually those who receive some KM team support and who nominate and train community hosts. Some people argue that the best groups 'just evolve'. This is true in some cases, but it is a high risk option for business critical knowledge sharing. It's fine to have a little formal behind the scenes effort to enable the informal contact to flourish. We call this being 'formally informal'. It is no different to splitting up groups onto different tables at events!

Make knowledge sharing part of the role

The GPLs and Sport champions were successful because they had knowledge sharing performance objectives, budget and a percentage of their time to devote to the role. Why leave something of strategic importance to the chance that people *might* have time to focus on it?

What we'd do differently

Use insiders

The KM team were careful about the language used but still had some credibility-busting moments (including an appearance in Private Eye magazine). Only two KM team members had programme-making experience but they were focused on developing social tools and did not work directly with the team members who provided internal consultancy. This hampered the consultancy side, who were criticised for marketing services and producing training materials that were 'not for' programme makers. Seconding staff members from the areas you are supporting to help translate into their local language is a much better approach. It also builds well-trained KM ambassadors in the business when their secondment ends.

Use a robust contact and stakeholder management plan

This ensures you maximise all interactions with staff potentially interested in knowledge sharing. In-house KM teams should think like an external consultancy group. The BBC's KM team didn't do this until the end. As they became overloaded with work they found that knowledge sharing between team members became difficult and opportunities were lost.

Up-skill your KM team at the outset

Analyse what is likely to be the predominant knowledge sharing solution used in your business, and provide KM team members time and resources to up-skill. The BBC's KM team needed to be well versed in CoPs from the outset. Whilst their learning grew over time, it meant the early adopters such as N&R Sport didn't benefit from some key learning. For example, the KM team discovered late on a key CoP statistic which is that only around 15–20% of your community will be regularly active at any one time. This is critical because, when trying to secure funding for community activities, many hosts set unrealistic expectations with their senior sponsors that large numbers of people will be active. If you set a target of, say, 50% of your invite list attending every community event over six months then you *will* fail as that is not statistically likely. This could have meant some CoPs failed at the first hurdle.

BP's Operations Value Process (OVP)

Operations Value Process (OVP) is the name given to the self-benchmarking process in BP operations. In this process each business unit measures itself against 6 key operational requirements or Expectations. These 6 key Expectations (shown below in Table 12.1) are further split into 26 key practices that are designed to deliver the Expectations. There is a further division which results in 78 elements with elements being how the practices are achieved. The hierarchy, shown bottom up is thus;

- 78 elements which deliver the
- 26 key practices which deliver the
- 6 expectations

Each operational business unit measures themselves against a series of set criteria on a standard form, for each of the 78 elements. This data entry form is available on-line and is normally completed by a cross section of people from the business unit, who hold a structured discussion and then award themselves a score for each of the elements (1 being low, 5 being high). This score is automatically rolled up to give a score for the key practices and then the expectations. The group also identifies the desired score that they wish to achieve for each of the elements. There will usually be a gap between the desired score, and their score of the current situation. This gap represents their desire to improve. It is worth noting that it isn't unusual for the group to decide that a current score is adequate and that they don't want to get any better at that particular element. In that case the discussion is about how to sustain that level of performance rather than improve on it. Once the gap between current and desired performance has been identified, a plan,

Table 12.1   Six elements and 26 key practices

1 Use the Right People and Processes	2 Cause no harm to people or the environment	3 Eliminate unplanned outages
Lead and communicate effectively Manage asset and organisational effectiveness Develop and assure competency Raise morale and motivation Drive performance improvement Share, transfer and embed know-how Enhance our reputation with community	Getting HSE Right Manage Greenhouse Gas emissions (GHG) Manage water	Manage production losses Exploit good reliability processes Manage integrity Operate equipment reliably
4 Effectively prioritise and execute planned work	**5 Optimise production**	**6 Minimise cost**
Plan, schedule and execute work Prepare and execute turnarounds	Optimise plant performance Satisfy customers Exploit advanced production technology	Manage OPEX budget Manage contracted (3rd party) services Manage process consumable costs Manage spare parts and stores Manage energy costs and efficiency Manage working capital

timeframe and owner for each element is created to close the gap (a KM plan, as described in Chapter 10 above).

For example, a manufacturing site using the Operations Value Process identified that it's current score was 1 out of a possible 5 (under their category 3: (Eliminating unplanned outages), element 3.2.4 (Failure analysis)) and that it wished to achieve a score of 3. The OVP system automatically provided a link to the toolbox element that can be used to close that gap. As discussed in Chapter 7, the toolbox is structured in a hierarchy of company standards and good practices, and in this particular example The Company Way contains a Group document which provides a standard approach to failure analysis. It also provides Good Practices for this topic such as a 'Root Cause Failure Analysis Manual' and another document entitled 'Using PowerPoint Organisation Chart to develop Fault Trees for RCFA.' So not only does the system provide a benchmark of your current position, it also provides you with tools to improve from current to desired position

One of the graphs created to help to compare the scores and gaps is the Staircase Diagram, an example of which is shown below.

Figure 12.2   **Staircase diagram**

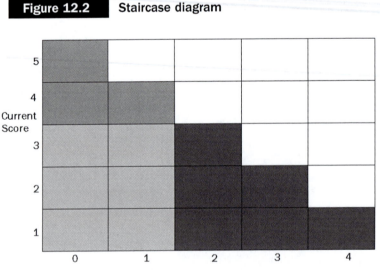

Current Score (y-axis): 1, 2, 3, 4, 5
Gap between current and desired score (x-axis): 0, 1, 2, 3, 4

This diagram showing the current score (vertical axis), versus the gap between the current and desired score (horizontal axis). Operational units in the green boxes have a high current score, while those in red have a low current score but a high desire to improve (large gap). The operational units in the red boxes can learn from those in the green boxes. The fact that they have identified a gap, suggests that they are willing to learn.

The advantage of the Staircase Diagram from a knowledge management perspective is that it allows these 'red box' units to identify the operational units who can be approached to assist them to improve, through sharing knowledge. The Staircase Diagram can also be used to identify areas that the company needs to improve on at a group or strategic level. For example if several businesses indicate that they wish to learn more about controlling emissions but there doesn't seem to be a 'best in class business' to learn from internally, they can form a Business Driven Action Learning team in order to learn from external organisations.

To ensure consistency across geographical and industry sectors, independent OVP assessors are often invited to participate in the OVP assessment. They provide challenge in a non confrontational manner, to make sure the teams don't over-rate their own current status.

Knowledge Management at CfBT Education Trust

By Carol Flach, Senior Knowledge Manager, Research and Knowledge Management Team, CfBT Education Trust.

CfBT Education Trust exists to provide education for the

public benefit. CfBT Education Trust has been providing education services and managing large government contracts worldwide for the last 40 years in Education ministries including England, Brunei, Malaysia, Qatar and Oman. We work with International agencies, including The World Bank, European Union and Department for International Development. In the UK we work for a range of government agencies including Ofsted, the Youth Justice Board, the National College for School Leadership and the Teacher Development Agency.

As a charity CfBT Education Trust is required by law to undertake activities that provide 'public benefit'. We do this in two ways: through client-funded activities that are of public benefit when they enhance the work of education professionals and the learning of students and through the re-investment of our surpluses in research that contributes to public benefit by creating knowledge of practical value to those engaged in education.

We work in more than 13 countries around the world including the UK. We employ more than 2000 staff worldwide and have an annual turnover that exceeds £100 million. CfBT Education Trust's growth had been rapid and undoubtedly successful, growing from a turnover of approximately £10 million in 1992 to £140 million in 2005. The increasing diversity of our portfolio, clients, locations combined with our research made it essential that we introduce an effective knowledge management programme. In April 2005 a small team was formed to help take the organisation on this journey.

Why introduce Knowledge Management?

Working with SMT (the senior management team), and with

external consultancy assistance, we set out to define what the scope and purpose of KM would be and to set out clearly the benefits that we were looking for. Initial examples of where KM had been introduced seemed to focus on process activities in areas such as construction where different teams carry out the same task many times. The theory and experiences from these sorts of organisations seemed at a distance from the reality of our complex and diverse organisation. Putting into practice our belief in knowledge management and trying to avoid the 'not invented here' mentality we set about identifying what from the industry standard approach could work (the learn before, during and after model, the collect and connect activities). From the beginning we were challenged to 'keep it real', identify what's in it for colleagues and most importantly to identify what difference it made. As educationalists and researchers there was a constant challenge for us to evidence base our approach. The environment into which we were seeking to introduce knowledge management techniques both supported and challenged us.

What worked and why?

One of the first things we did was set KM within the context of what we called Corporate Learning. Corporate learning took a wider view of the need to demonstrate to clients, beneficiaries and trustees evidence of what worked and why. Our approach to KM was two pronged:

- To carry out centrally led assessments and evaluations to identify impact and the factors that contributed to it, then to distil and distribute the learning from them.

- To stimulate local learning and accumulation of knowledge by creating a network of Knowledge

Champions embedded within the various teams and locations across the organisation.

There is no doubt that the first of these strands was easier to organise and yielded quick and useful wins, the latter was and is a much longer and harder journey for us as a client-focused people-centric organisation.

We are still very much in the infancy in terms of embedding and systematising knowledge management. The second strand of our approach requires us to embed a learning culture in the way we work and to establish the role of Knowledge Champions within all our operating teams. Both of these tasks take time and need encouragement and reinforcement.

The twin tracked approach set out a targeted series of interventions for knowledge capture and learning and a universal element. Centrally targeted assessments and evaluations, good practice events, learning reviews (retrospects) were relatively easy to organise and beneficial but sometimes were seen as bolt-ons and in an organisation with a central head office and a dispersed workforce there was sometimes a cultural barrier and resistance to 'central initiatives'.

At a time of great change within the organisation we were keen to ensure that we sought to align and link with other management information initiatives and business improvement initiatives. The year from April 2005 to 2006 was one in which several changes took place within the organisation. The Chairman of the Trustees had recently changed and the sponsorship and challenge from the new Chair John Harwood was invaluable in terms of profile and focus. The introduction of a balanced scorecard approach to management information enabled us to embed within this the need to report on and therefore to have in place systems for objectively assessing how effective we are at consciously capturing and sharing our learning across the organisation.

Figure 12.3   **Balanced scorecard**

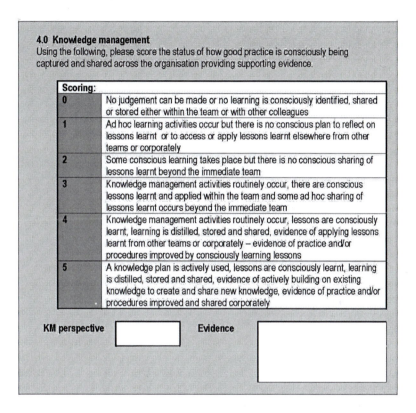

What else worked?

Much of our business is secured by competitive tendering. The main customer for our knowledge activities and evidence of good practice was and continues to be those responsible for maintaining our market share and growing our business through competitive tendering exercises. Clients consistently challenged us and others in the education market to demonstrate the impact of our work, knowledge management was one tool we used to identify and gather together practitioners to identify what worked and why. Good practice events and events that sought to identify the impact of government policy on our offer were very well received and effective forums for distilling our learning in particular areas of expertise. Whilst the language of the 'Knowledge Exchange' has never quite made it in to general conversation, the activity of gathering together our leading expertise in symposium format is becoming routine and part of how we do business.

What were the challenges and how we sought to address these?

Much of our work is carried out in partnership with organisations who are sometimes partners, sometimes competitors and sometimes the client. This adds a further degree of complexity to our work and to the introduction of knowledge management activities. Culturally it has not always been possible to involve valuable contributors to activities in knowledge reviews due to the fluid nature of relationships and the barriers between clients/contractors and partners/competitors.

The sheer range of knowledge within CfBT Education Trust is remarkable. There are individuals and teams who know how to:

- Educate some of the most troubled young people in the UK
- Reform an entire education system in the developing world
- Turn around failing schools

- Train a generation of future leaders for England's schools
- Change the behaviour of teenagers in Africa to reduce the chances of HIV-AIDS transmission.

In addition to our specialist educational areas of knowledge, we also have lots of leading-edge knowledge in vital generic areas such as:

- Project management
- Client management
- Events management
- E-learning
- Materials development

Within the generic areas many teams have developed bespoke tailored offers that map to the exact requirements of the client and beneficiaries. Offering a tailored and personalised learning outcome is core to the way in which CfBT Education Trust differentiates itself from other service providers who do not necessarily have an exclusive focus on education. In these circumstances innovation and application are core competencies which we do not wish to lose. It was therefore essential to position KM as an activity that would increase the opportunity for innovation and maximising impact and not reduce it through a one-size-fits-all template approach.

Our overriding concern has been to generate and support the right sort of environment for knowledge sharing.

We can't all be an expert in everything but we are all an expert in something!

It doesn't make sense to start an activity anew each time when you know someone out there must have done it before, or sometimes it would be nice to have some advice from someone else who's been in your situation. But who do you ask, or where do you go to find out something?

CfBT Education Trust road show flyer (April 2005)

Meeting the needs of a diverse audience

Within every company there are colleagues who seek out the technology solution and those who are people-centric and want as much face-to-face time as budgets and time allows.

Access to lessons learnt and case studies of effective practice was a key issue for us. It was a key part of our communication plan for us to develop a Corporate Learning intranet site to store the lessons learnt from retrospects and after action reviews. It was essential for us to store not only the knowledge assets but also to route core information and cross company business improvement projects within the same site so that colleagues wherever they are in the company can see that we are interested not only on the learning points for individuals but also for wider application across the organisation.

Figure 12.4　**CfBT Education Trust Corporate Learning intranet**

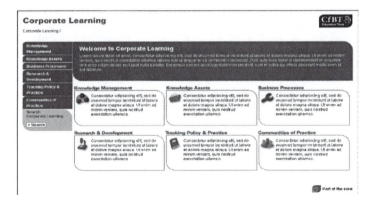

Training

Initially we trained a core of Knowledge Champions using an external training course. This was well received but we were keen to ensure that future training was based on the model of knowledge management that we had developed for CfBT Education Trust.

Extract from Knowledge Management Training for CfBT Education Trust staff

Section 2: Using Knowledge Management within CfBT Education Trust

Learning outcomes

- Understand the relevance of KM for CfBT Education Trust

- Consider the advantages and challenges

- Identify current systems and processes

Training coverage

- Why is KM important for CfBT Education Trust

- Individual – employee and beneficiary

- Organisation

- Where are we now and where do we need to be?

- Barriers to knowledge exchange

- Creating Communities of Practice

- The role of Knowledge Champions
- Capturing data
- Using common language for KM

Section 4: Action planning for KM

Learning outcomes

Consider how to apply this training to their practice, including for:

- CfBT Education Trust as a whole: leadership and responsibilities, communication, training, involving beneficiaries and clients
- Departments/teams: roles and responsibilities, team development, Knowledge Champions
- All practitioners within CfBT Education Trust: CPD and Action Planning
- Creating a personal KM action plan.

General Motors

Adopting and Adapting Product Best Practices across General Motors Engineering Six Years Later, by Steven Wieneke, GM Technical Fellow, Global Technical Memory, Global Engineering, General Motors Corporation

Background

This case study examines how creating a Technical Memory has enabled the Subject Matter Responsible Engineers to connect with the Design Engineers and has allowed them to grow the number of Approved Best Practices from zero to over 4000. The cost avoidance for applying Best Practices is measured in millions of dollars. Product Engineering now has a visible learning process to ensure GM's Intellectual Capital is current and relevant. Sharing, adopting and adapting these practices across GM Global Engineering are now integral to the way they work. The case study also outlines how product quality has dramatically improved, time to market has been accelerated and structural cost has been reduced. The engineering culture is reported as progressing from hoarding to sharing knowledge and from re-inventing to adopting and adapting what is already known.

> General Motors Corporation ... the world's largest automaker, has been the global industry sales leader for 75 years. Founded in 1908, GM today employs about 327,000 people around the world. With global headquarters in Detroit, GM manufactures its cars and trucks in 33 countries. In 2005, 9.17 million GM cars and trucks were sold globally under the following brands: Buick, Cadillac, Chevrolet, GMC, GM Daewoo, Holden, HUMMER, Opel, Pontiac, Saab, Saturn and Vauxhall.
>
> http://www.gm.com/company/corp_info/profiles
> (September 2006)

2005 was one of the most difficult years in General Motors' 98-year history. It was the year in which GM's two fundamental weaknesses in the U.S. market were fully exposed: our huge legacy cost burden, and our inability to adjust structural costs in line with falling revenue. The challenges we cited in this space a year ago – global overcapacity, falling prices, rising health-care costs, higher fuel prices, global competition – intensified and significantly weakened our business ... we are changing our business model to deal with the larger phenomenon of globalization and the competition it has brought to the U.S. economy. We already have made some significant moves to improve our competitiveness in the long term. We need to do more – and we will.

Letter to Stockholders, Rick Wagoner, General Motors Corporation, http://www.gm.com/company/investor _information/docs/fin_data/gm05ar/content/letter/letter_ 01.html (September 2006)

The knowledge initiative described in this case study does not directly address the current challenges facing General Motors. This initiative combined with others implemented within Product Engineering in the 2000 timeframe have and continue to contribute to reducing structural costs, improving product quality and competitiveness.

Issue & challenges

General Motors conducted an enterprise wide investigation early in 2000, and found six systemic issues that would be resolved under the 'Quality as a Value' project. One of the systemic issues was not having a comprehensive set of documented product engineering solutions and supporting product best practices. This issue was assigned a significant portion of the 2000 annual warranty and campaign

144

expenses. The assignment was to document key product best practices across all aspects of the vehicle as quickly as possible without sacrificing the quality (inclusiveness, relevance, accuracy) of the content.

The decentralised product engineering organizations prior to early 1980s were autonomous. The pervasive cultural was one of hoarding knowledge. Engineers were rewarded for their knowledge and know-how. In the early 1980s GM began a series of North American Product Engineering reorganisations and most recently consolidations, from 5 groups to 2 and finally 1. With each organisational change many of technical references became obsolete or were discarded. Knowledge was 'managed' primarily in a tacit-to-tacit exchange through mentoring and on-the-job training. During the mid to late 1980s, the Truck Engineering organisation would double in size. Car and Truck Engineers were regularly rotated 3 times into 3 year assignments within their organisation to gain cross function experience.

In June 2000, GM embarked on a strategy of supplementing existing engineering tacit knowledge with structured explicit knowledge around all aspects of the product. This explicit knowledge documents what engineering solutions work; why, where and when the solution works and who reviewed. This strategy consists of 2 parallel activities one creating and sustaining a Catalog of Engineering Solutions and the other Technical Memory – Best Practices. The combined objective is to improve product quality, reduce structural costs, and improve time to market. Secondary anticipated outcomes are growing engineering know-how and improving work task effectiveness and efficiency. This case study addresses our progress in creating and sustaining an engineering culture of sharing, adopting, adapting and applying product Best Practices.

When an enterprise is unaware of the importance of balancing tacit and explicit knowledge, the enterprise is left vulnerable in several ways. First, when most of the core business knowledge is tacit, knowledge is often lost through employee attrition or related cost saving measures. Second, when the core business knowledge is primarily explicit, there may be very little employee *know-how* or depth of understanding. If the enterprise has minimal explicit knowledge, the enterprise will have no alternative but to deploy their experts to mentor and troubleshoot while sacrificing new product development, creating appropriate explicit knowledge or keeping abreast of technological advancements. Maintaining a balance between explicit and tacit knowledge is essential to the success of any enterprise. (Wieneke and Phlypo, Knowledge Management Domain, General Motors Corporation, October 2003, p. 9)

Implementation timeline

This case study presents the chronological events from initiation to present. The events were tailored to the journey at General Motors Product Engineering and not necessarily in the order that would be repeated if implementing in a different organisation or culture.

June–December 2000

The first 2 steps of eventually discovered 9 steps were already in place in June 2000. First, there existed a mature product centric taxonomy made up of 2 perspectives. The first perspective reflects the physical product and is referred to as the Bill of Material (BOM). The other perspective reflects product performances like Initial, Long Term and

Perceptual Quality; Fuel Economy; Ride; Handling; Crash Avoidance and Protection; etc.

Second, approximately 12–18 months earlier our Engineering Executives identified Subject Matter Responsible Engineers (SMRE), one from car and one from truck engineering, for each subject. Subjects are generally the second level of the taxonomy. For example, a first level BOM Row is Chassis. Examples of Second Level Rows are Front Suspension, Rear Suspension, Steering, Frames, etc.

Additionally, prior to June we had successfully delivered to the Chassis Frame Design Engineers' desktop a web-enabled, manufacturing design-rule database. The Truck Chassis Engineering organisation had participated with a consortium organiser, a vehicle frame supplier, and 2 universities to compile manufacturing and welding rules for truck frames. To ensure a consistent and comprehensive collection of rules from multiple sources, we created a structured format for collecting the rules. The rules were eventually captured in a knowledge base and dynamically presented as virtual documents. The intent was to grow this knowledge base with a sufficient number of engineering rules to *drive* an existing parametric chassis assembly consisting of parametric components. The parametric model of the truck frame alone required over 3500 parameters to define a true geometric, solid model instance of a design. We knew besides the geometric rules that by necessity had been programmed into the parametric solid model, that there were 4–6 other rules (or perspectives) for each parameter that would need to be considered like manufacturing, assembly, safety, durability, etc. The knowledge base was the scheme to manage all of the potential rules.

The success and learnings from this pilot were used in designing and implementing the current Technical Memory

– Best Practices knowledge base. The structured content of our current Best Practices is detailed as part of the sixth of eight disciplines of a proposed model of the Knowledge Management Domain. (Wieneke and Phlypo, Knowledge Management Domain, General Motors Corporation, October 2003, pp. 13–15.) Figure 12.5 illustrates the What-Why-When-Where-Who structure of the GM product Best Practices.

Figure 12.5   GM product best practice structure

The product Best Practice content is written knowledge (what, why, when, where and who) about product design features and the subsequent produced performances.

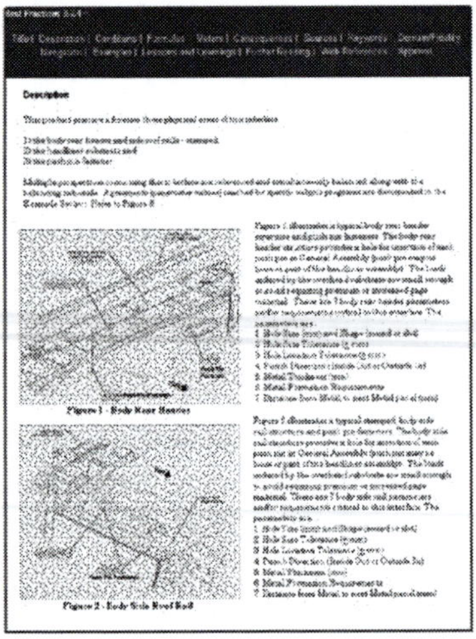

Best Practice Sections	Inclusiveness
1. Title & Abstract	What
2. Description	What
3. Conditions	Where & When
4. Formulas	What (Math)
5. Performance Meters	Success Range
6. Consequences	Why
7. Sources	Who
8. Key Words	Search Tags
9. Examples	Proof of Re-use
10. Supporting Data	Lessons/Learnings
11. Approval	Who

Using the taxonomy and designated SMREs, we published a Roster and initially chartered, across 33 Centers of Expertise, 138 Best Practice Teams to begin authoring Best Practices. We then brought the 200 SMREs together for a kick off meeting using the Paramount Pictures *Mission Impossible* movie trailer as the theme. Their *assignment* was explained along with supporting testimonies from their peers explaining why they needed to begin documenting their knowledge about the product. Expectations, timelines, metrics, templates, examples and team coaching were provided over the next several months as well.

During the first 6 months we conducted approximately 300 two-hour long coaching sessions providing instructions on what a product Best Practice is and is not, demonstrating the differences between Best Practices and other technical sources like procedures, requirements and specifications. We described the various types of Best Practices, provided a method to prioritise what should be written. Several of the teams adopted project management techniques recording each Best Practice to be written the assigned Author(s), date of each Best Practice State (Draft, Submitted, and Approved) as well as technical review dates.

We deliberately limited the scope of a Best Practice to 5–6 related design parameters, a *nugget of knowledge*. Limiting the scope allowed the SMRE to write a Best Practice over the course of 40 hours while working on other assignments. The limited scope additionally increased the likelihood that a group of peers could review, agree and technically approve the Best Practice in a timely manner. These technical reviews would prove to be the most time consuming aspect of the process. SMREs that had focused primarily on troubleshooting often had difficulties initially describing what works and why. Their starting point was always from *what is not working*. Through coaching and inquiry, sometimes with the presence of physical hardware, the SMRE would move to a preventive mindset and begin authoring Best Practices.

January–December 2001

The internally developed Best Practices knowledge base went into production early in January 2001. Best Practices that Authors had written using a temporary MSWord template were manually entered into the knowledge base. The entire first year only focused on the Authors and their progress in completing approved Best Practices. The initial focus was on addressing product quality and warranty. The monthly metrics reported during this period were the number of Best Practices written to the number of Best Practices identified. Each team established their own monthly targets. Coaching continued and an ACCESS database was created to record and report each team's progress and provide the team leader with the next series of steps (a prescription) to be completed before the next coaching session. Teams typically required 3 coaching sessions with assigned tasks between sessions to become self sufficient.

Figure 12.6   Graphical domain view example

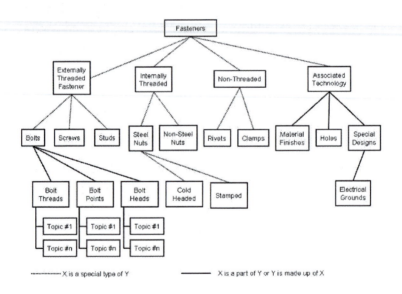

To determine the number of Best Practices identified we developed a method to graphically model the number of Best Practices for an area of practice called a 'Domain View'. Figure 12.6 contains an example of a graphical domain view for one area of practice, Fastening. An additional metric was created to track the progress of each team's Domain View. During the first six months, the state of the team's domain view was reported from the bare minimum of a simple list to an outline to a graphical depiction accompanied with an authoring project plan.

Best Practice Author and Approver coaching continued. The role of Knowledge Asset Manager (KAM) was defined to assist with coaching and electronically approving the Best Practices. The KAM became the end-of-line quality check for Best Practices. The Technical Memory Team facilitated monthly KAM meetings providing training, answering frequently asked questions, sharing successes, and conducting software user clinics. Each Center Director assigned this role to one of their SMRE or an individual familiar with the product and engineering business processes. Eventually we provided examples of the best written Best Practices.

During the same period that we were refining the role of SMRE to include defining engineering solutions and writing Best Practices, GM began the process of merging the car and truck engineering into one engineering organisation. The cultures were different as well as their engineering solutions.

January–December 2002

The focus again for 2002 was on the Authors and their progress in completing approved Best Practices. The Best Practice content now includes focus on product competitiveness as well as quality and warranty. During

2002 over 1800 Best Practices were written increasing the number of approved Best Practices from 687 to 2522. The number of Authors and Reviewers increased from 200 to approximately 600, teams increased from 116 to 143, registered users from 1046 to 3045. Refer to Table 12.2, refer to Accomplishments, for additional metrics and trends for 2001 through 2006.

Two new challenges surfaced during the second year. Up to this point, there was no attempt to reach agreement on best practices across functional areas. The Best Practices the SMRE wrote were *free expression*, typically heuristic in nature and from a single perspective. With 2522 approved Best Practices, there were several examples of what appeared to be *conflicting* practices. Actually, each practice would prove to be true from a functional area perspective but *competed* with other functional areas. For example, General Assembly might require a flange to be as wide as possible and the Mass Group would prefer the flange to be narrow.

This first challenge was addressed by developing a formal collaboration process which allows each cross-functional area to write about a mutually agreed upon engineering solution (includes nomenclature, illustrations and datums) from their functional area perspective. Using a graphically presentation method, refer to Figure 12.7, the cross-functional perspectives are balanced and the balanced solution is captured in a *balanced* Best Practice which has precedence over the single-perspective Best Practices.

The facilitated collaboration process is summarised in Figure 12.8. To enable this process, we developed and piloted a custom software application that would *harvest...*

- the relationship between topics to be collaborated (i.e. knowledge structure),

Figure 12.7   GM Product Best Practice Meter Stack
(R, red; Y, yellow; G, green)

The final value of a design parameter is not necessarily a discrete, single value. A continuum of values typically exists for each design parameter. In a GM product Best Practice this continuum is displayed as a Meter consisting of combinations of Green, Yellow and Red Zones. The Green Zone is intended to be values where the design performs without additional considerations. The Yellow Zone is intended to be values where the design performs with additional considerations. The Red Zone is intended to be values that should not be considered due to practicality or physics. Each Meter represents a single perspective unless labeled Balanced. The Balanced Meter is constrained by the single perspectives and inherits all of the additional considerations from any overlapping single-perspective Yellow Zones.

- the mutually agreed upon engineering solutions,
- the associated nomenclature, illustrations and datums,
- each functional area's perspective
- any functional area additional considerations and
- the final balanced solution.

We successfully demonstrated that the harvested information and knowledge could be uploaded to the knowledge base as draft Best Practices for the SMRE to embellish and publish.

The formal collaboration process had several unintended positive outcomes. Since each perspective was captured and each affected SMRE participated in the balancing decision, confrontation between SMREs disappeared. In fact, many SMREs indicated that they were learning and looked forward to the next facilitated session. We attribute this learning experience to spending time at the beginning of the

| Figure 12.8 | Facilitated Best Practice collaboration process |

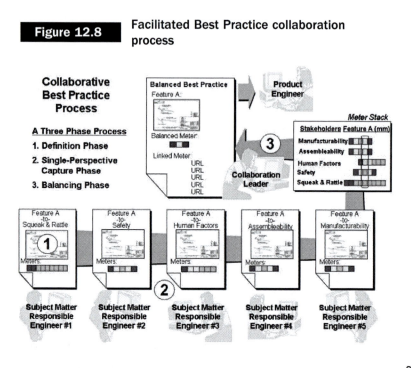

22

collaboration to verify the participants understanding and agreement on nomenclature, illustrations and datums. We have found the graphical presentation method, shown in Figure 12.7, to be universally understood and the final outcome is most often self evident.

Our second challenge was to devise a method for bundling and delivering groups of Best Practices to the appropriate Design Engineer. Authors deliberately wrote limited-scoped Best Practices (nuggets of knowledge) therefore several Best Practices would be required to design a component or subsystem. Our solution is a Knowledge Set, refer to Figure 12.9, an electronic 3-ring binder containing...

- *how-to* instructions,
- a list of linked Best Practices (what, why, when, where and who),

- linked short-cut access (View Meter button) just the engineering product rule, and

- a list of linked other technical resources like procedures, specifications, references.

Figure 12.9   Knowledge Set

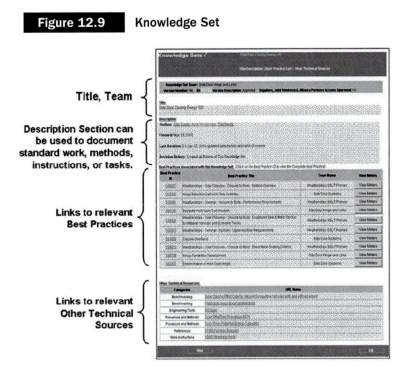

January–December 2003

At the beginning of 2003 there are 2522 approved Best Practices with an additional 856 added that year. Engineering Executives directed our focus from Authors to the Design Engineers who will be adopting and adapting the Best Practices. We change the reported metric from the number of Best Practices written to the monthly average number of daily user sessions, as well as minimum and maximum number of sessions for each month. A user session or visit is measured in 30 minute intervals; logging in and out 2 or 3 times within 30 minutes only counts as one session. A user session will generate multiple database *hits* each time a piece of data is pulled from the database to create the virtual document. The number of *hits* is related to how the data has been configured and presented and is not a meaningful user session metric.

We continue publishing the annual number of approved Best Practices written and identified by each Center (ranked contribution). We also began the process of globalising the Best Practice content and the user base.

By the end of third year, writing and sharing Best Practices is an integral part of the SMREs job, which is reflected in their performance reviews, part of the GM Performance Management Process (PMP). Management uses the PMP in determining salary merit increases and bonuses. Management also provides multiple opportunities for additional exposure for these individuals with cross-functional leadership where the SMRE may present existing knowledge and new learnings through venues like 'Learning Days', Quarterly Best Practice and Learning Communication Meetings or SMRE communication meetings.

January 2004–December 2005

We continue to focus our efforts on the Design Engineer adopting and adapting Best Practices. To communicate the significant cost avoidance achieved by applying Best Practices we publish vignettes. The vignettes consist of a title, a knowledge quotation, representative illustrations, a description of the situation or scenario and a summary of cost avoidance typically measured in millions of dollars. In May 2004, Technical Memory is endorsed by Global

Engineering Executives as the single, global repository for engineering product knowledge.

The metric changed from the number of user sessions to the number of Best Practices viewed by region. Reviewing Table 12.2, refer to Accomplishments, reveals that the 36,553 Best Practices viewed in 2003 increased to 119,334 by the end of 2005. The percent of Best Practices viewed by Author/Reviewer and Design Engineer remains effectively constant for 2003 through 2006, at 16% and 84% (±2%), respectively. Consistently at least one third of the Best Practices are revised each year. The Design Engineer's standard work now includes applying Best Practices. Design and peer reviews are used as the means to ensure Best Practices or a validated engineering solution has been applied.

The next and continuing challenge is to ensure Best Practices and other technical sources reflected the most current new learnings and preventions for lessons. We delineate between lessons and learnings. Lessons are *things gone wrong* and have been corrected. Learnings are *things gone right* that we want to adopt and adapt (reuse). For the lessons, we want to capture the preventions not the corrections. Corrections are not necessarily the best means of prevention.

An internal audit of the North American lessons learned process revealed the lessons were not being consistently addressed. In April 2004, the lessons learned process was replaced with a visible learning process called 'Closed-Loop Learning'. The Closed-Loop Learning Process ensures that actionable preventions and learnings are inserted into General Motors' Intellectual Capital for future adoption and adaptation by any employee. Intellectual Capital is divided into 3 categories;

- Technical Excellence (individual know-how)

- Intellectual Properties (Best Practices and other written technical resources), and

- Technical Exchanges (key meetings where information and knowledge is exchanged).

Any engineer at any time can bring a prevention for a lesson or a new learning to the appropriate subject matter responsible team(s). The Closed-Loop Learning Process ensures that GM reuses learnings and avoids repeating lessons. GM learns. The closed-loop part of this process, or the ultimate closure, is when someone other than the initial learner repeatedly and consistently avoids repeating a lesson or appropriately re-applies valid and relevant knowledge. The North American Lesson Learned database is decommissioned on January 3, 2006.

January–December 2006

Year six executive mandate is to globalise our engineering solutions and Best Practices across all regions. This process initiates around the global a new wave of training in all of our knowledge tools and processes. The opportunity of improving the fidelity of the Best Practices from heuristic to experimental or scientific is now possible as a result of the extensive Design for Six Sigma training and project completions across product engineering. The number of Best Practices viewed continues to increase around the global and appears to have reached a steady-state level in North American. Viewing metrics for 2006 are 168,777 Best Practices viewed.

Accomplishments

1. Technical Memory has enabled the connection of Design Engineers with Subject Matter Responsible Engineers by publishing Rosters in Global Technical Memory and the web-enabled, enterprise-wide organisation chart.

2. The global subject matter responsible engineers have grown the number of Approved Best Practices from zero to over 4063.

3. The cost avoidance for applying Best Practices is measured in millions of dollars.

4. Product Engineering has a visible learning process to ensure GM's Intellectual Capital is current and relevant.

5. Sharing, adopting and adapting these practices across GM Global Engineering are integral to our jobs.

6. Although not solely a result of this initiative...
   a. product quality has dramatically improved
   b. time to market has been accelerated, and
   c. structural cost has been reduced.

7. The engineering culture is progressing from hoarding to sharing knowledge and from re-inventing to adopting and adapting what is already known.

Figure 12.10 summarises the annual business metrics used to track the completion and viewing of Best Practices and Knowledge Sets. The metrics used throughout this activity where non-invasive and directly related to the tasks.

Figure 12.10	Best practice and knowledge set annual overall metrics

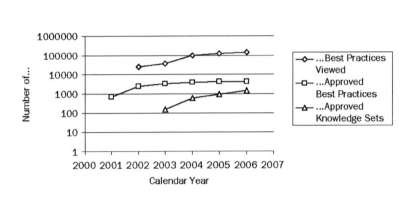

Table 12.2	Technical memory – best practice annual metrics

			End of Year, Number of...				
Year	Best Practice Teams	Registered Users	Approved Best Practices	Identified Best Practices	Approved Knowledge Sets	Avg. Daily User Sessions	Best Practices Viewed
2001	116	1046	687	6168	NA	NA	NA
2002	143	3045	2522	6294	NA	1842	25 508
2003	173	NA	3378	3529	149	4200	36 553
2004	200	NA	3777	5351	602	4761	96 423
2005	225	NA	4013	6096	907	NA	119 344
2006	262	11 000	4063	6059	1443	NA	168 777

The Annual Overall Number of Best Practice Viewed, shown in Figure 12.10, is broken down by each of the 4 global regions in Figure 12.11. Figure 12.12 illustrates the ratio of users and authors viewing Best Practices for 2006. There has been a significant focus during 2006 to train engineers outside of GM North America to structure their product knowledge for sharing and reuse and author Best Practices.

Figure 12.11   **Annual number of best practices viewed by global region**

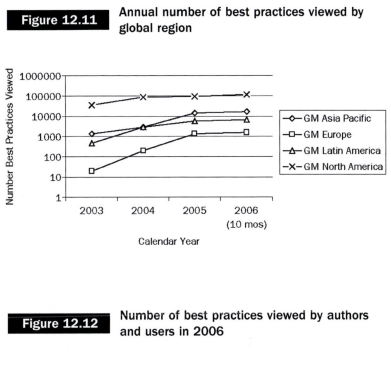

Figure 12.12   **Number of best practices viewed by authors and users in 2006**

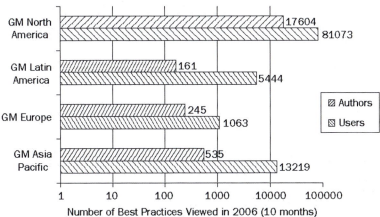

Business metrics that affect the financial bottom line (like reduced warranty cost, improved JD Power and Consumer Report rankings, etc.) can only now begin to be considered due to the inherent 3 to 6 year lag between action (design) and outcome (customer using the product). As previously stated, 'This initiative combined with others implemented within Product Engineering in the 2000 timeframe have and continue to contribute to reducing structural costs, improving product quality and competitiveness.'

Figure 12.13 illustrates the decreasing (normalised) 36 Month-in-Service (MIS) Actual Warranty to our Reduction Warranty Forecast. The Actual 36MIS curve stops at calendar year 2003 because the data cumulates over 36 month intervals and is just now available in 2006. The Catalog of Engineering Solutions, Best Practices, Knowledge Sets and the Closed-Loop Process are 3 of the current 10 sustained activities identified as Engineering enablers for exceeding the warranty reduction guide path shown in Figure 12.13. As more and more Best Practices are adopted and adapted, and the other activities continue successfully, General Motors intends to surpass our warranty reduction forecast.

Learnings

The knowledge tools and processes that were implemented worked. The key to success has been continuous communication at all levels, connecting the Design Engineer with the SMREs, the perceived value of the Best Practices, a structured approach rather than free format for knowledge capture, face-to-face coaching with Authors and Users, peer testimonials and vignettes, and most importantly successful designs.

Figure 12.13 Normalised 36MIS Actual Warranty and Warranty Forecast

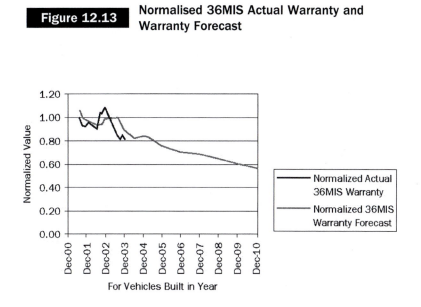

For future implementations, I recommend the emphasis should be on implementing a visible enterprise-wide learning process rather than lessons learned or best practices. The learning process will necessitate identifying existing intellectual capital which eventually justifies creating and maintaining intellectual properties like best practices.

Documenting what you know does as much for the Author as the end user by surfacing and clarifying what is known and most importantly the why's, when's and where's. The Author reaches a level of awareness which should help them be better mentors and teachers. The documentation becomes secondary.

An initiative of this magnitude must include an adequate IT maintenance budget to maintain the production knowledge tools/software as behavior and business processes change. Behavioral changes must always lead IT solutions, but the IT solutions must be ready as the organisation matures and adapts.

We found the following 9 steps essential for implementing and sustaining an enterprise learning process are...

1. Create Taxonomy by Area or Community of Practice (CoP)

2. Identify Subject Matter Responsible Person for each CoP

3. Make Communities of Practice visible

4. Identify key individuals (the main internal customer) in each CoP

5. Make visible what the CoP must know

6. Make a Intellectual Capital Ledger visible for each CoP
   - Technical Excellence (Education, Training, Mentoring)
   - Intellectual Properties (Best Practices and other written technical sources)
   - Technical Exchanges (peer assists, after action reviews, peer reviews, Design Reviews)

7. Identify sources of lessons and learnings for enterprise (long-term emphasis should be on learning, innovation, invention)

8. Make the Enterprise Learning Process visible

9. Leverage Metaknowledge (knowledge about knowledge) Practitioners

Next Steps

- Complete the globalization of Best Practices and other technical sources.

- Improve the fidelity of Best Practices using Design for Six Sigma methods, and

- Continuously refresh Best Practices and other technical sources resulting from new learnings and preventions for lessons.

- Integrate a more inclusive and explicit *what-is-known* mindset into the Best Practice content structure.

Orange

By Debbie Lawley, previously Head of Organisation Learning and Knowledge, Orange Group, now Director of Willow Transformations

The Mobile Industry

The traditional mobile operator business model is becoming more unsustainable. Subscriber growth has flattened as penetration climbs above 100%. High subscriber acquisition costs (principally as a result of handset subsidies), high churn levels and falls in the price per minute of mobile voice telephony are placing severe pressure on operators' margins.

It is argued that mobile operators have handed too much power over to intermediaries, who make their living from commissions on selling new handsets and contracts (and are therefore incentivised for moving customers from one operator to another). Operator marketing and subsidies have encouraged a situation where handsets have become a fashion item with customers looking to replace their handsets an average of only 13–15 months. Consequently, operators are looking to deal with more customers through their direct channels and where possible decrease subsidies and commissions and increase the length of subsidies.

Over 70% of operators' revenues come from customers making voice calls, this is becoming a commodity. The average price of voice services has been falling and is expected to continue to drop. This is a highly competitive market, very volatile. The market deals directly with leading edge technology breakthroughs combined with fashion trends making it also very unpredictable.

Orange has been a leading part of this market since its launch in 1994. It is a fast moving business reflecting the rapidly changing nature of mobile telephony. The handset is no longer just the device to take and make calls. Today people use their mobile to text, to retrieve voice mail, to browse emails, calendars, to look up information on the internet. The degree of complexity in supporting the Orange customer is greater than ever.

Orange was purchased in August 2000 by France Telecom. This formed a mobile group of some 14 companies and started a major rebranding exercise across a substantial footprint. The Knowledge Management challenge in this environment is tremendous, from product knowledge and innovation through to professional knowledge and knowledge in how to support the Orange customer in the best way possible.

The particular challenge in the Call Centre of fast moving companies

The Knowledge Management team had a clear role of helping Orange get value from its knowledge – the importance of the link between learning, knowledge sharing and knowledge building. This was especially critical in this fast moving organisation. A great example of this in practice is the Call Centre environment. Call Centres are fascinating places. Every change that happens in the company comes home to roost in the Call Centre at the point of contact between the representative and the customer. Every technical change in products, every technical change in support IT, every campaign launched, every tariff change made. This is a true knowledge challenge. It is the ability of the representative to have the right knowledge presented in the right way for the best conversation with the customer that matters so much in establishing customer satisfaction, a critical benchmark of KM success.

Coaching in Call Centres – the Community model in the UK

In January 2003, the approach to learning changed in the Call Centres in Darlington. The Head of Call Centres, UK, made the decision to adopt a community style approach.

The Coaches to the Representatives were originally in the reporting lines of each of the teams. The business driver of customer satisfaction meant that this had to change. With a reduction in staff as well, the coaches were pulled out of the teams and placed together.

Their remit was to improve the performance of the Call Centres through improved learning. Their target was to improve customer satisfaction. They had to achieve this by working with those who had the intimate knowledge of the customer – the Call Centre Representatives themselves, especially the experienced ones, plus the staff who assess customer feedback and those who handle customer survey information.

What happened?

Communities are different to line management organisations – they put knowledge at the centre of the community and then are flexible but focused in how they maximise the benefit of knowledge to the benefit of the participants and the organisation.

In this case study, the community involved the coaches themselves, the experienced Representatives, the staff who assess customer feedback and satisfaction plus the customers themselves through survey data. Together they were able to establish what mattered to the customer and what actions were likely to improve the customer's experience.

They met together, reviewed the information together and created insight from their knowledge of what was happening on the line. By sharing insights and reviewing the data collectively, they were able to target initiatives to achieve rapid improvement.

The Community together assessed the feedback from Orange customers, plus the insights of the experienced Representatives to create initiatives such as the 'empathy' scheme, to give the Representatives the understanding of how to handle situations where the customer may not be happy with the service.

The typical features that characterised this community were a strong common purpose, trust and openness, minimal hierarchy and intense knowledge sharing. In this community, some people had a specified role – the coaches, others participated actively – the customer satisfaction staff and experienced Representatives, and others contributed just as valuably, but passively – the customers themselves through their feedback.

The results in accelerated in customer satisfaction, were almost immediate.

Training coaches in community leadership

The Community Supervisors quickly realised that their traditional management style would not work. The success of the new arrangement depended on giving the coaching community the room to use their imagination to create the very best means to accelerate learning across the Call Centre. A new style of facilitation was required in this new way of working which differed dramatically from traditional line management.

This new style of working was supported by a training programme for the people who now found themselves as community facilitators. A workshop was to cover a number of key concepts around community working, with each section using exercises to consolidate learning by applying the techniques explored to produce materials for their community:

- *Communities: definition and case studies.* In order to help delegates understand how a community differs from other organisational designs, how and why they are used and the success factors for communities in Orange.

- *Communicating community purpose to sponsors and participants.* A clear purpose related to the needs and challenges of the particular business area/professional discipline is vital to secure the buy in needed for a successful community. During the early stages of the course, the delegates were asked to work with each other to create a purpose statement for their community, from both the participants and sponsors view.

- *Exploring types of communities.* After providing delegates with a definition and examples of the four main community types (helping, best practice, knowledge stewarding and innovation), they were encouraged to reflect on their community and explore which elements of these community types were relevant for theirs.

- *Community roles.* Exploring the various roles needed to sustain community activity helps delegates to understand with whom they need to engage to secure sponsorship, develop a core active membership, identify subject matter experts and over time, how to sustain activity and engage less active participants. This also includes understanding their role as the community facilitator.

- *Community facilitation skills.* Understanding the difference between facilitation and other modes of working, in particular leadership or direct management helps to explore the key competencies and skills needed to be a successful community facilitator. This includes giving practical examples of the type of activities a community facilitator will be involved in on a day to day basis.

- *Enabling technology.* As a large complex organisation, a key driver for communities is to make available the dispersed knowledge and experience for anyone who would benefit. Therefore, it is necessary to provide supporting technology to enable these exchanges to happen regularly, to be easily captured and then shared. In addition, understanding the technological enablers also allows communities to make the most of face-to-face events by encouraging relationship building, direction setting and discussion rather than report or document sharing.

- *Benefits analysis: exploring benefits of communities over time.* Orange is a complex, task-focused organisation and as such, communities need to be closely aligned to business need. The benefits analysis exercise gives delegates the opportunities to explore how their community will provide benefit to their four key stakeholders; members, sponsor, the line managers of the members and their customers/clients. We also explore how these benefits will change over time, because this helps facilitators articulate the journey of the community from research, through to creation and nurturing and onto action and commercial benefits, gaining vital support from sponsors through this process.

- *Community action planning.* Having explored their community in depth over the course of the workshop, delegates are then encouraged to devise a 3 month action plan detailing the steps they will need to take to launch their community, including key events, communications planning and ongoing day to day activity.

The workshop had to be highly practical and include time spent working on the delegate's actual community issues. Delegates were given many opportunities throughout the workshops to develop materials and resources specifically for their community. Exercises were based on their community concept, not on hypothetical models. The objective was to complete the first steps towards community launch when they left the course.

The knowledge benefits tree

The results were immediate, with a steady increase in the customer satisfaction figures in the following months after the community was put in place. The figures increased from 69% to 76%, a remarkable achievement; primarily achieved it is believed through the change in coaching style. Other internal figures also improved.

The outcome of improved customer satisfaction through improved knowledge flow within the Call Centres also impacted the Key Performance Indicators. An interview technique was used based on a method documented by

Figure 12.14   The Knowledge Benefits Tree

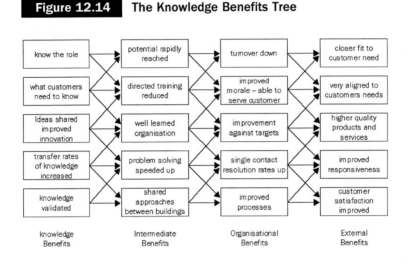

know the role	potential rapidly reached	turnover down	closer fit to customer need
what customers need to know	directed training reduced	improved morale – able to serve customer	very aligned to customers needs
Ideas shared improved innovation	well learned organisation	improvement against targets	higher quality products and services
transfer rates of knowledge increased	problem solving speeded up	single contact resolution rates up	improved responsiveness
knowledge validated	shared approaches between buildings	improved processes	customer satisfaction improved
knowledge Benefits	Intermediate Benefits	Organisational Benefits	External Benefits

Skyrme to capture the relationship between the improved knowledge flow and the results in other Key Performance Indicators. The results are mapped out in the benefits tree shown as Figure 12.14. The Community style approach meant that the coaches had properly understood their role; they understood what the customers needed to know. They were sharing ideas with each other, transferring that improved capability across the Call Centres and validating to ensure that change had the desired impact. This meant that people were reaching their potential more quickly, problem solving was speeded up and the same approaches were being shared across the different buildings.

The organisation benefited through reduced turnover of staff, improved morale because people felt better able to serve the customers and the single contact resolution rates increased. The customers were receiving better service, they felt they were getting a more responsive and empathetic response from the representatives and they felt more satisfied with Orange as a result.

There were still some sticking points; like how to address

the need for immediate help for the Representative with a customer on the line. They also faced difficulties with career progression. The result of all this was to move to a hybrid model over time, where coaching communities are used in anger where the knowledge needs are highest.

The Belgian example – process and community link

The Belgian operation was a typical example of learning communities in action. The role of the coach is seen as crucial to the effectiveness of Call Centres but can only achieve so much in terms of improvement if regarded as an isolated role. Trainers are responsible for the knowledge base, which holds explicit information that Call Centre employees refer to. Again, a crucial role but of limited effectiveness if seen as an isolated role.

The Training Manager in Belgium analysed knowledge gaps through wrongly assigned calls. The Training Manager looked for causes in the knowledge gap but explicit knowledge may not be the only solution. By setting up a learning community made up of coaches in the call centres, trainers and product managers, it was possible to assess the real cause of the knowledge gaps and jointly design and implement interventions. By working as a community with a common goal (product managers are rewarded on revenue), the knowledge of the call centre staff was reviewed from different perspectives and enhanced through the most appropriate means. This included 'knowledge islands' where the coaches work with two representatives and also coach each other.

By introducing communities, the knowledge base, both explicit and tacit is constantly renewed. As a result a true learning cycle is created by using a mix of techniques and perspectives to assess problems, implement solutions, validate and review the outcomes.

The Belgian Call Centre approach features in the 'Orange – learning whilst doing – guidelines'.

The Mobistar's 'coaching and learning whilst doing' Example

Mobistar CSRs are each entitled to 4–5 coaching sessions per year. The coach uses evidence from the calls analysed by the NICE tool as the basis of the coaching session. During the session, the coach and coachee explore 3 key questions:

> What will I continue to do?
> What will I stop doing?
> What will I change?

The answers to these questions will help the coaches to design their own action plan (with guidance from the coach) to enable them to achieve the desired results. The action plan will then be reviewed and updated at the next coaching session.

Technology

The role of training and learning specialists in managing K Village.

One of the greatest risks and areas for unique advantage in call centres is excellent access to accurate and timely information. With the degree of rapid changes, this is especially challenging in a call centre environment. In 2005 there were some 98 new releases of products, services and tariffs to the UK Call Centre.

Products in a telco environment are released with the tightest timescales, they have to be. The training cycle then is exceptionally short. The trainers are usually scheduled to receive the product 2 weeks before release and often those timescales are less. Training large call centres of many people becomes very challenging. The idiosyncrasies of the product will not become apparent until it has been released and used in large numbers in the field and in all environments.

In Belgium, the training and learning specialists are responsible for the content of K Village – the web site for call centre representatives. By using the community approach, feedback from the field, the knowledge gaps and the immediate learning experience from the customers are all fed into the web and constantly updated and replaced.

The role of e-learning and knowledge nuggets

Getting new knowledge across widely dispersed audiences rapidly, cheaply and effectively is demanding. Both retail and call centres suffer from similar dispersal issues plus the need to flex around rota's and slack times.

E-learning is widely employed in Orange and increasingly so, in getting small knowledge nuggets of new information out to the people who need it to do their jobs. The new information comes from the new services and products plus the learning experience from practice.

What did we learn

Communities can be an incredibly useful technique in understanding how to engage people together in targeting a joint goal. In a call centre, it represents a means of gathering insight from different functional areas and using that explicit and implicit knowledge to target much more focused actions that have rapid effect in achieving the business goal of improved customer satisfaction. Part of the issue in a call centre is the difficulty of getting over the very constraints the organisation puts in place – such as keeping people at their desks taking calls instead of reflecting on experience and collectively working together to improve outcomes. Additionally, insight tends to be dispersed into different functions with separate groups holding insight into survey information, others having product knowledge, still others holding insight into the issues customers are facing now.

The community aspect is one useful technique – reviewing the knowledge needs in terms of a flow of knowledge that many different people contribute to, can be even more effective. In the case of the Belgian operation, they had created a system where the trainers, the product managers, the coaches, the representatives all understood their roles in the learning cycle. A process was put in place to include refection on symptoms of knowledge gaps and all the appropriate roles played their part in closing the gap, all under the umbrella of a community.

Communities are especially useful in the way they focus upon the key target that the team were striving for. The benefits tree helps to put in perspective the way in which the 'efficiency targets' also improved as a happy outcome but not as the key driver. So often these are the very targets which are seen as the end goal and the knowledge goal is lost along the way.

What we would you do the same and why

It is rare to find KM initiatives that bear such rapid results. Because of the proximity of the call centre staff to the customer, it was perfectly possible to get results in days of making the community centred changes. This is very inspirational! Recognising the role of the coach, not as a deputy line manager, but as someone who is responsible for customer satisfaction through improved knowledge was key. So was pulling a community together that maximised insight into customer satisfaction, something the organisation usually is designed to avoid!

The other key attribute of knowledge in a call centre and in fact knowledge in many parts of an organisation, is that it is emergent. The launch of a new product to business customers is just the start in understanding that product. The performance of that product in the 'field' starts a whole new process of understanding about that product and its features and how customers choose to use it. The explicit mechanisms we use frequently assume a more static nature to that knowledge. Use of collaborative software, such as wikis, to capture emergent knowledge about products in action are an interesting new development opportunity and one which will probably be much more reflective of how we work and learn, especially in a call centre environment.

What would you do differently and why

Battling with other initiatives – initiative exhaustion

One of the big problems in call centres is the sheer number of competing initiatives all coupled with a drive to cut costs. The emphasis all too easily becomes one where the efficiency of running a call centre is the target, not the target of satisfying the customer. It takes energy and commitment to overcome this from the top. Call centres do seem to attract multiple initiatives from HR, technology, facilities – you name it! This brings about initiative exhaustion in a big way and blurs understanding.

Metrics

Although many things are measured within a Call Centre environment, the main or top level metric is Customer Satisfaction. The following diagram shows how Customer Satisfaction rose as the UK Call Centre move implemented a learning based community model in 2003.

Figure 12.15   Customer satisfaction metrics

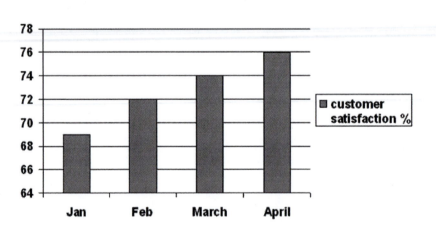

Conclusion

In conclusion, we found that having run a successful KM program that there were six questions that we would encourage anyone who wanted to replicate our success to consider. By being clear on the answer to each of these questions you will be better able to plan the introduction, target your resources and measure the impact that you are making. Measuring the impact you are making is important as it allows you to correct your course as you progress.

The questions that you should be able to answer are:

1. What is the key target?
    i. (what is it you want to change or improve)
2. Who is responsible for the key target for this area?
    i. (who is the gatekeeper or person who must be engaged to allow or enable that change)
3. How is knowledge and learning embedded in roles at present?
4. How is that knowledge kept current and available at present?
5. How do they currently spot knowledge gaps?
6. How will you track improvement?

    i. How will you know that you are making an improvement?

Summary and conclusions

This book has been a detailed walk-though of knowledge management as it applies to the services, operational and manufacturing environments, and it's a lot to take in. This final chapter will use the knowledge management cycle to summarise the main conclusions.

Strategy

- You don't have to manage all the knowledge that your company possesses, focus on the key knowledge.
- Use different approaches to managing knowledge that has low or high value.
- Use different approaches to managing knowledge that you know a lot about versus knowledge that the company has little experience of.

Communities of practice

- The explicit corporate knowledge base is held in the company's standards, operating procedures and best practices.

- The community of practice holds the tacit knowledge base and plays a key role in ownership and transfer of knowledge.

Review

- Learn from the success of your own performance.
- Conduct a performance learning review.

Benchmark

- Performance measurement allows an operation or production unit to track it's performance levels, measure your current performance.
- Benchmarking allows it to compare those levels with other units, and identify the areas where it needs to improve, or areas where it can help others improve.
- Target setting allows it to focus on areas for improvement, establish a target for future performance.
- Targets are generally lower than the performance already achieved elsewhere.
- Knowledge management allows it to acquire or develop the knowledge it needs in order to improve.

Learn

- Create a knowledge management plan to identify the key knowledge you will need.

- Learn from others, use a process such as the peer assist to learn from others.

- Visit another site and use the site knowledge visit process to learn from them.

- Conduct a knowledge exchange where there are multiple locations to learn from.

Do

- Access the local and corporate knowledge bases and lesson learned databases.

- Use the after action review process to capture your learning as you go.

Roles

Clear roles and accountabilities are needed in any effective knowledge management system. These roles might include:

- Corporate knowledge manager.
- Team knowledge manager.
- Knowledge management sponsor.
- Community facilitator.
- Knowledge management coach.
- Subject matter expert.

Assurance and monitoring

If the cycle of learning and performance is to be maintained, the company must have some way of monitoring and assuring that this cycle is being applied effectively to improve performance. This assurance may have the following components:

- Knowledge management standards.
- Knowledge management plans.
- Knowledge management monitoring.

References

Clemmons Rumizen, M. (2001) *The Complete Idiot's Guide to Knowledge Management*. Penguin Putnam.

Collison, C., Parcell, G. (2004) *Learning to Fly: Practical Knowledge Management from Leading and Learning Organizations*, 2nd Bk&Cdr edn. Capstone.

Confederation of British Industry (1999) *Knowledge Management, A Real Business Guide*. London: Caspian Publishing Ltd.

Davenport, T. H., Prusak, L. (2000) *Working Knowledge*. Harvard Business School Press.

Dixon, N. M. (2000) *Common Knowledge: How Companies Thrive by Sharing What They Know*. Harvard Business School Press.

Gorelick, C., April, K., Milton, N. (2004) *Performance Through Learning: Knowledge Management in Practice*. Oxford: Butterworth-Heinemann.

Harvard Business Review on Knowledge Management. Harvard Business School Press, Library of Congress Card Number: 98-234096.

Milton, N. *Knowledge Management for Teams and Projects*. Oxford: Chandos Publishing.

Nonaka, I., Takeuchi, H. (1995) *The Knowledge-Creating Company: How Japanese Companies Create the*

Dynamics of Innovation. Oxford University Press.

Schien, E. H. (1999) *Process Consultation Revisited, Building the Helping Relationship.* Addison Wesley Longman Inc.

Stewart, T. (1997) *Intellectual Capital: The New Wealth of Organizations.* New York: Currency/Doubleday.

Appendix 1

Forthcoming publications

We started this series of books by looking at knowledge management for teams and projects. We then moved on to looking at knowledge management within a services, operations and manufacturing environment. The next book in the series will share our insights on knowledge management in sales and marketing environments. If you would like to contribute to the book, either in the form of a case study or your experience within that environment, please contact Tom Young at tom.young@knoco.co.uk

Index

AARs, 62
ACCESS Database, 150
Accomplishments, 159–62
After action review, 21–5
Assurance and monitoring, 103–6

BBC case study, 74, 95
BBC Production and Services, 119–30
  The Champion Model, 121–2
  KM training, 122
  The Sport Community launch, 123–6
  N&R knowledge-sharing matures, 126–9
Benchmark, 182
benchmarking data, 14
benchmarking process, 34, 130
benchmarking, 15, 19–20, 60
  Internal, 15
Best Practice Replication (BPR system), 73–4
Best Practices knowledge base, 148–9
Best Practices, 154–9, 162

Bill of Material (BOM), 146
Blogs, 90–1
BP Operations Excellence toolkit, 76
BP Q&A system, 88
Business driven action learning, 60–3
Business knowledge manager, 95
Business metrics, 162

Call Centre Challenge, 166–77
Case histories, 119–80
CfBT Education Trust case study, 74
CfBT Education Trust, 79, 106, 133–42
Chassis Frame Design Engineers, 147
Closed-Loop Process, 162
Communities of Practice (CoPs), 120
Community facilitator, 96–7
Community leadership Training, 169–71
Community, 65–72

of purpose, 68
of practice, 68–70
of interest, 71
tools and processes, 71–2
Community, of practice, 73
CoPs, 129
Corporate knowledge
manager, 94
Corporate Learning intranet
site, 140

DaimlerChrysler model, 71
DaimlerChrysler, 71
do/review cycle, 9

eClips Community
discussion forum, 76–7
eCLIPS system, 77
eCLIPS, 76, 88–9
eLearning, 86–7
e-learning, the role of,
175–8
Engineering Book of
Knowledge (EBOK), 73
explicit, 4–5

General Motors case study,
98
General Motors, 142–65
Issue & challenge,
144–5
Implementation timeline,
146–59
Accomplishment, 159–62
Learnings, 162–5
Geographical Information
System, 2
Good practices, 76, 120
Gorelick, 6

GPLs, 122–3, 125

Health, safety and
environmental (HSE)
management, 115–16
Hybrid search, 81

ISO system, 111

K Village, 79
Key Performance
Indicators, 171
Keyword search, 81
KM team, 119, 123, 125
KM Training, 122
KM, 135
know-how, 3, 65
Knowledge asset manager
(KAM), 98, 151
Knowledge benefits tree,
171–3
Knowledge exchange,
45–60, 138
Knowledge management
coach, 96
Knowledge Management
Domain, 148
Knowledge management
monitoring, 105
local operational unit,
105
community of practice,
105–6
within organisation,
106
Knowledge management
sponsor, 95–6
Knowledge management,
17–20, 103, 166

question and answer forums, 87–9
Question and Response system, 76

Reconvene and feed back, 55–6
Risk assessment, 115
Risk management, 113–15
Roles, 93–102, 183

Sigma-Connect system, 84
Sigma-Connect, 85
Site knowledge visit, 34–44
Six sigma, 107–9
SMRE, 148–9, 151–3, 156, 162
SON&R (Sharing Opportunities Across Nations & Regions), 126
Sport Good Practice Champions, 123
Stages, knowledge exchange process, 46–60
setting up, 46–51
format, 51–6
Recording, 56–9
Output, 59–60
Stages, Site knowledge visit, 34
Set-up, 35–40
Knowledge transfer, 40–1
Debrief, 41–4
Staircase Diagram, 132–3
Stewart, 68
Structure, knowledge exchange, 45–6
Subject matter experts, 97–8

Subject Matter Responsible Engineers (SMRE), 147

tacit knowledge, 32
Tacit, 4–5
Takeuchi, 4
Target setting, 16–17
Technical Memory, 147–8, 156
Technology, 79–92
The Belgian example, 173–4
The BP Way, 76–7
The Closed–Loop Learning Process, 157–8
The corporate knowledge base, 73–8
The General Motors case study, 118
The Mobile Industry, 165–79
The North American Lesson Learned database, 158
The Orange case study, 67
The Sport community launch, 123–6
total cost management (TCM), 110
total quality management, 111–13

Wikis, 91–2

yellow pages system, 84
Yellow pages/people finders – see Yellow pages, 84–5

standards, 103–4
plans, 104–5
monitoring, 105–6
metrices, 106
Knowledge Set, 154–5, 159, 162
knowledge, 4–5
K-Village system, 67–8

Leaders (GPLs), 120
Lean operations, 109–11
Learnings, 162–5
legal services context, roles, 98–100
    Professional Support Lawyers, 99
    Professional Support Paralegals, 99–100
    Know-How Partners, 100–1
    Librarians, 101
Lessons Database, 74
Lessons learned databases, 81–4
Librarians, cybrarians, 98

management disciplines, links, 107–18
Menu search, 81
Metrics, 178
mineralogical data, 2
Mobistar CSR, 174
Month-in-Service (MIS), 162

Nonaka, 4

operations technicians, roles of, 100–2

Operations Value Process (OVP), 130–3
Orange Call Centres, 79
Orange case study, 96
Orange, 165–79

Peer assist, 31–4
    Structure, 32–3
Performance benchmarking, 13–20
Performance measurement, 13
    benchmarking, 13
    target setting, 13
    knowledge management, 13
performance learning review (PLR), 10, 25–30
Performance learning, 21–30
    After action review (AAR), 21
    Performance learning review (PLR), 21
    Performance Management Process (PMP), 156
Performance management, 116–18
Pipe inspection, 33–4
Portals knowledge libraries – see portals, 79–81
Prusak, 6
Prusak, Larry, 5

Quality System Management Standard, 111